EVELYNE ACCAD was born [...]
Francophone literature at the U[...]
the United States. *Wounding Words*, her third novel, is preceded
by *L'Excisée* (L'Harmattan, 1982) and *Coquelicot du massacre*
(L'Harmattan, 1988). She is also the author of *Veil of Shame:
The Role of Women in the Contemporary Fiction of North Africa
and the Arab World* (Naaman, Sherbrooke, 1978); *MontJoie
Palestine! or Last Year In Jerusalem* (a translation of a dramatic
poem by Noureddine Aba (L'Harmattan, Paris, 1980);
Contemporary Arab Women Writers and Poets (with Rose
Ghurayyib, IWSAW, Beirut, 1985); *Sexuality and War: Literary
Masks of the Middle East* (New York University Press, 1989).
The French version of *Sexuality and War, Des femmes, des
hommes et la guerre*, won the Prix France-Libano in 1994.

DR CYNTHIA T. HAHN, Associate Professor of French at Lake
Forest College, Illinois, researches and publishes in the field of
Francophone literatures, specialising in French-Canadian and
North African women's writing. She has received AIMS
(American Institute of Maghrib Studies) and university travel
grants for trips to Tunisia to research the Tunisian women's
movement in recent years. She holds a Doctorate in French
Literature from the University of Illinois (Urbana) and a Master's
degree from Purdue University, Lafayette, Indiana.

EVELYNE ACCAD

WOUNDING WORDS
A Woman's Journal in Tunisia

Translated from the French by
Dr Cynthia T. Hahn

Heinemann

Heinemann Educational Publishers
Halley Court, Jordan Hill, Oxford OX2 8EJ
a Division of Reed Educational & Professional Publishing Limited

Heinemann: A Division of Reed Publishing (USA) Inc.
361 Hanover Street, Portsmouth, NH 03801–33912, USA

Heinemann Educational Books (Nigeria) Ltd
PMB 5205, Ibadan
Heinemann Educational Botswana (Publishers) (Pty) Ltd
PO Box 10103, Village Post Office, Gaborone, Botswana

FLORENCE   PRAGUE   MADRID   ATHENS
MELBOURNE   AUCKLAND   KUALA LUMPUR   TOKYO
SINGAPORE   MEXICO CITY   CHICAGO   SÃO PAULO
JOHANNESBURG   KAMPALA   NAIROBI

Blessures des Mots: Journal de Tunisie
© Indigo & Côté-femmes éditions
This translation © Cynthia Hahn 1996

First published by Heinemann Educational publishers in 1996

Series Consultant: Abdulrazak Gurnah

British Library Cataloguing in Publication Data
A catalogue record for this book is available from the British Library.

ISBN 0 435 905236

Cover design by Touchpaper
Cover illustration by Helena Greene

Phototypeset by CentraCet Ltd, Cambridge
Printed and bound in Great Britain
by Cox & Wyman Ltd, Reading, Berkshire

96 97 98 99 10 9 8 7 6 5 4 3 2 1

For Amel Ben Aba

*For Ilham, Rashida, Hayet, Siham, Alia,
Khedija, Harfidha, Nora, Jalila, Hédia,*

*and for all the marvellous women of Tunisia
who have led me on this journey.*

1

The Mediterranean sparkles at her feet. A Tunisian Nefertiti claims the beach, arms outstretched, thick hair curling in all directions. Stepping carefully on round pebbles, Aïda moves in harmony with nature, breathes deeply. Profiled by the setting sun, she challenges a darkening sky. Her body claims its freedom, breasts uncovered to the wind.

A call to Gaïa. Aïda raises her arms, capturing the enchantment of this place. Inhaling slowly, she lowers her arms, then lets out a long breath. The tranquility of the moment calms her to quiet meditation. It gives her peace and fills her with energy.

Aïda enters the water and, breathing in deeply, shakes off her fatigue. Her hands, which were stretched skyward in a sacred gesture like the goddess expressing her vitality to women, now break the waves, pulling her body towards the horizon. She swims, following the disappearing sun, then returns to the beach with long strokes. Pulling her bathing suit over her chest, she leaves the water as a magical apparition, shimmering droplets streaming in symmetry.

> Woman of Tunisia, breasts naked in the waves
> Unthinkable
> Woman of Tunisia, alone in the sea at nightfall
> Inconceivable
> This woman, though, is present – alive
> Borne up by her dreams
> Crying out her burning desire to live, her thirst for
> freedom
> A call for justice, an unmasking of oppression
> Her movement communicates itself
> Her wave generates other waves

1

Crest after crest raised
Stir the sea in its depths
It rolls, rolls over polished pebbles
transformed to fine sand.

Aïda runs towards the house on the shore. The door is ajar. She enters the small garden, calling, 'Hayate, you should have come with me. It was magnificent!'

Hayate comes out, tray in hand. She sets it on the table and smiles to see that Aïda is radiant in the twilight, her eyes gleaming. 'I'm glad you could relax after such a heavy day ... you've been so tired lately. I went swimming earlier. Come and have tea with me; I'm so glad you could come over.'

Aïda shakes her dripping hair, dries herself. Hayate pours the tea ... on the tray are rolls, butter, apricot and fig jams. Aïda's daughter, Saïda, asks for a piece of bread and jam. Hayate pours the milk and makes her a snack which she devours. Salty air stimulates the appetite.

Aïda lets out a sigh of well-being and lights a cigarette. 'It's so good to be here. I've washed off all the dust and worries of Tunis. I would love to be able to live close to Nature all the time, to the sea, the earth and the sky. It gives me unbelievable energy. The trees pass on to me their peaceful and majestic strength. The flowers flood me with their scent and colour. The birds tell me fabulous stories in a language that makes me dream. The sound of the sea cradles and comforts me.'

Hayate watches her with affection, and lights a cigarette as well. 'The sea has a power to renew that always surprises me. I chose to live here for just that reason, even though for a woman alone, staying in such an isolated house by the sea is risky.'

Aïda sighs deeply: 'We should assert ourselves and not be afraid any more. If we don't, who will? Your presence here in Tunisia has taught me a lot.'

'I learn from you, too; you give me such energy, courage, hope.'

They gaze at each other and then turn to the sea which has taken on deep blue hues with the approach of night.

2

Aïda continues to speak as if pursuing an inner monologue: 'Men are destroying the Earth with their weapons of war. I wish I could tell them to dive into the sea, without fear and not in a spirit of vengeance and conquest, so they could see the marvels the sea creates. They would come out transformed and decide to end pollution and destruction. If they learned to love Nature, they would also love women better. They would encourage them to blossom.

'I'm becoming more and more aware of just how much the patriarchal system is built on the exploitation of Nature,' Hayate adds, her thoughts in unison with Aïda. 'Men reinforce their strength by subjugating Nature just as they do women. Love for Nature works like a salve on wounds men inflict. If only we could communicate some of this love!'

Aïda stands up: 'I'd love to be able to talk with you for longer. I never tire of our conversations. They nourish me and help me to move forward without fear, to assert myself . . . but I have to go before nightfall. Will you come to the Club tomorrow?'

'Yes, of course. I'm having lunch with Rima in the souks. We'll be there around four o'clock. Do you know what the plan is?'

'We'll be organizing the International Day for Women, then we'll discuss the connection with sexuality. There will be some personal accounts, I think. In the evening, there will be a meeting at my house to plan our new journal. Why don't you come? You could spend the night at the house. We'll have more time to talk then.'

'I'd love to come. I'll make a Lebanese rice dish if you like.'

Aïda bursts out laughing: 'You're always thinking about food – that's great! Come,' she says, taking her daughter's hand, 'we've got to go.'

Hayate accompanies them to the train. The little blue and white station at Salammbô is welcoming, with its stone benches, the red light of the evening tinting them rose and mauve. The train pulls in slowly, not very full at this hour.

Aïda resembles a gypsy with her large flowered skirt, her mass of uncombed shining black hair, a bouquet of wild flowers in one

3

hand and her daughter on the other side. What a miracle of freedom, such a ray of light in this stifling society! They turn to each other and embrace in silent understanding.

Aïda and her daughter wave as the train departs. Night is falling rapidly. The air is cooler. Hayate takes the alley where Nayla lives. The window to her room is lit.

'Nayla, Nayla!'

Nayla opens the window and recognises her. 'Come on up for a cup of coffee.'

She climbs the stairs. Nayla waits for her at the door, an awkward smile spreading over her face. She invites her into the room. Her bed is disappearing beneath books and magazines. The walls are covered with posters and photos, calling for the liberation of the oppressed. She puts on a record, a song by Jacques Brel.

She seems very excited and speaks rapidly:

'I'm so pleased you're here! You must help me! I'm preparing an article on women textile workers in the area. Their working conditions are inhumane. They have to be talked about, even if it's dangerous. If we don't have the courage to reveal injustice, who will? People are so apathetic!'

Her voice reveals her enthusiasm. She fidgets about while speaking: 'Come with me and bring your tape recorder and camera if you like. I don't know if we'll be able to get in, but it's worth a try.'

She turns the record over. A young woman comes in with small cups of steaming coffee on a tray. She sets them down on the table and leaves. Nayla hands her a cup. 'Sugar; a cigarette?'

Hayate opens her bag: 'Here, have an American one!'

'No thanks, Hayate! I like the Tunisian brands, and from time to time a Gauloise, but American, no . . . well . . . maybe I'll try just one.'

Nayla's hesitation and change of heart amuse Hayate. She knows about Nayla's horror of American products, like a good number of left-wing Tunisian intellectuals, yet she is surprised by the outright rejection of everything American, while with France,

4

the relationship is subtler, more complex. Protests made by the American grass-roots movement which asks the same questions, fights for the same causes, are unknown here. Hayate understands how one can detest American politics, but this over-simplification astonishes her.

She can't explain these feelings to Nayla. Nayla intimidates with her incisiveness, her categorical expression of ideas. Violent affirmations always leave Hayate speechless. She looks toward Nayla, who doesn't notice that she is ill at ease and is now furrowing through her magazines and records. She puts on a song by Edith Piaf:

> Non, rien de rien, non je ne regrette rien!
> Tout le mal qu'on m'a fait, tout le bien
> Tout ça m'est bien égal!

She approaches Hayate with a pile of books and magazines in her hands.

'Here! Take all these! They should interest you. There are studies of Tunisia, articles I've written on the bread riots, the Southern miners . . . Here, do you know this novel about Lebanon, *La Citadelle d'Osta* by Leïla Osseïerane translated from the Arabic by Marie-Thérèse Arbide? And this book by Raymond Jean: *Lettres de prison de Gabrielle Russier*, the story of that woman who wanted to live differently, and was finally pushed into suicide by society? We can discuss them when you've read them.'

With her hands full, Hayate feels wrapped in love and attention. She gazes at Nayla with affection.

'Thank you, Nayla. I'm looking forward to reading them. I'll bring these books back next week when I've finished. Are you coming to the Club tomorrow?'

'I don't know. I have a lot of work. I have to prepare this article, a paper for my classes . . . and besides, I've had enough of the Club. Too many fruitless discussions . . . and, I've got to take care of my mother . . .'

Hayate gets up to leave: 'Let me know when you want to go to the textile factory. That really interests me. Now I have to go home, before it gets too late. Do you have a bag for all these books?'

Nayla gives her a plastic bag. Hayate stands up, fills the bag and hugs Nayla. But Nayla steps back, as if embarrassed by the display of affection. She turns abruptly and heads toward the door. Hayate follows.

In the next room, her mother is sitting in darkness in a wheelchair. Petite, shrivelled, her bones visible through her skin, paralysed from head to foot, she can no longer speak. Upon seeing Nayla, her face lights up, her eyes sparkle.

'Mama, I'll walk her back and buy you the biscuits you like and some cigarettes.'

Her mother attempts a smile. More like a grimace. Hayate goes close, squeezes her hand, very small, emaciated. She hesitates, moved at the sight of this tired hand, this face marked with suffering. Her eyes fill with tears before this vision of wounded humanity.

Nayla helps her. She takes a cigarette, lights it and puts it in her mother's mouth. After many contortions, she is able to take a few puffs. Nayla asks the young woman to keep an eye on her. Her voice becomes gruff: 'All right, let's go! I'll walk with you for a bit.'

They go down quickly. Hayate is unable to shake off her sadness. Nayla reproaches her: 'How sentimental you are! Go on, there's no need to be so sad!'

Hayate looks at Nayla who is taller by more than a head. She has such a lively, excited way of talking about her projects. Her body, on the heavy side, seems to hold back her enthusiasm. Her abrupt and clumsy manner hides a great timidity, an extreme modesty. Hayate is filled with admiration for her courage, her tenacity, her determination to pursue her studies, various projects and political commitments all at the same time, and to care for a mother requiring constant attention. Hadn't she seen her one day carrying her mother by herself up the stairs? At this thought, her eyes fill with tears. Nayla puts an arm around her shoulder. A protective gesture.

6

'What's wrong, Hayate? What's the matter?' she asks.

'Oh, it's nothing! I was thinking of the day when I saw you carrying your mother – such a small package of bones in your strong arms! You were climbing the stairs under her weight!'

Nayla shakes her head, surprised. Hayate wipes her eyes and tries to control her sadness by thinking of other things.

'Nayla, are you writing?' she asks.

'You always ask me the same question. Yes, yes, I'm writing. I'll show you the text as soon as I'm ready. I'm dragging pages out of myself, pages I should have written a long time ago, writing that your visit has triggered. Yes, Hayate, I am writing. It's hard and painful, but I'm writing.'

Then her face grows sombre. It is as if she regrets her confession. Once again, she rushes on: 'It's already dark, you'd better go. I'm going to stop in here for some biscuits and cigarettes. Go on, go ahead . . .' With a hurried wave, she moves away.

Hayate returns home following the shoreline, the sea fixed in blackness. The wind has died down and there are very few lights on this part of the coast, just several boats and fishermen. Again, a sharp feeling of anguish and melancholy grips her. She pushes open the garden gate, opens and then double locks her apartment door. Through the open window comes the sound of waves dying on the shore.

She thinks of all the Tunisian women she has just met, those she is beginning to get to know. She admires them and senses her growing attachment to them.

> Women walking in the brambles of uncleared paths
> Women skinning their hands on walls that encircle them
> Women singing through the darkness of their time
> Women crying out so that others may hear the call
> Women writing to denounce fear, cowardice, injustice
> Women living differently, with difficulty
> So that others may see the light

Take up the flame
Spread warmth everywhere
And the waves, waves rolling to infinity
Plaintive song of a sea in eternal rebirth

2

Hayate awakens and is filled with wonder at the sound of the waves she never tires of hearing. This tumultuous movement reassures her, even though the wind unleashes itself and the turmoil intensifies. This feeling of travelling – this secret of her life woven by departures and arrivals – excites her with the conviction that time is short and there is so much still to accomplish.

She makes a cup of coffee and sits under the arbour. There is her diary to write. The sea is calm, shining under the sun's rising. Hayate notices how quickly the sea changes colour! With the passage of just one cloud or one gust of wind, it spans all the shades of blue, green, silver, gold or violet. Nature's transformations are in harmony with her deepest being, searching for subtleties. At this hour of the day, the sea is made of silver. Hayate opens her diary, writes down her first impressions of her arrival in Tunis.

> City phosphorescent blue and white
> Scent of pressed olives and harissa
> The damp dust of your walls clings to the skin
> Like the insistent eyes of your men
> On women's bodies and faces
> Violent glances which incite revolt
> Cries of rage, a call to action,
> A walk in the forbidden city,
> A table in barred restaurants
> In forbidden cafés
> A seat in prohibited movie theatres
> Solidarity of women appropriating spaces closed to
> them.
> Screams over screams, rediscovering the echo
> Thousand-year-old howling of slaves

Médina labyrinth of my heart
Meanders of my past bleeding from its wounds
Souks, arcades, the pulsing of a lost Beirut
Eye of henna-stained hands
Kohl of my scars
Incense of my suffering
I would like to engrave forever
A time which will not return
The story of these women
Silent and strong
Daring to challenge.

Now the sea takes on a reddish hue. A grey-mauve mist rises from the water, firing the horizon. Hayate closes her diary, puts away her cup and leaves with a large overnight bag.

She walks happily to the train station, feeling light and full of joy, humming the song by Brel that she heard at Nayla's the day before. She steps past dustbins invaded by hungry cats who scarcely notice her presence.

Nayla's window is wide open. She calls up to her. No response. Then the young woman who had served them coffee the previous day appears on the balcony. She gestures towards the station. Nayla must have left for Tunis.

Hayate rushes to buy a newspaper and a ticket, and boards the train. There are over a half a dozen small stations between Salammbô and Tunis. They all resemble each other, quaint, bright blue and white, round polished stone benches and ivy on the walls, waiting for flowers. Hayate is struck by the cleanliness compared to the trains and stations of Paris and its suburbs. And they say the Third World is dirty!

Hayate enters a compartment, takes a spot on the bench seat and scans the newspaper. Always the same headlines: Bourguiba is well. He took his morning walk, met with the Minister of Foreign Affairs, gave a speech. His prime minister Mzali held a reception, visited some city or other. Lebanon. Still just as sombre. Still the same horrors. Car bombs, a dozen killed, Israeli bombings in the South. Visits to Damascus by delegates of different Lebanese parties. Reconciliation is impossible. Refusal to negotiate ... familiar news.

It plunges her into painful reflection: where are the solutions when every country in the world fuels conflict with weapons in order to boost its economy? And the Lebanese! They cannot put their differences aside, differences anchored in religious fanaticism derived from a feeling of tribal pride. They do not unite in a shared love of country, chase away the occupying forces, reject those who fight for territorial dominance, rise up against all who fan the flame of dividing up countries.

Hayate puts down the paper and studies the countryside which moves her with its beauty. The sea wall. The train cuts across the sea; there is water on both sides. On her right, an expanse of still water, covered with seaweed, filled with birds, long, graceful, shifting lines of white, mauve, grey. On her left, the port – pleasure boats, fishing vessels, freighters, warships. Heavy steam rises from the engines. Hayate wonders how she could have lived far from the Mediterranean for so long and if she will be able to leave it again.

Tunis. Everyone leaves the train. Hayate is swept up in the anxious crowd. She breaks away and walks quickly up Bourguiba Avenue, the pedestrian-only square at the centre with a statue of Bourguiba on horseback and great arteries of traffic to the right and left, bordered by trees, flower sellers and newspaper vendors.

She arrives at the International Hotel and goes to the overcrowded café, packed with men. Packed with men who stare at her. Persistent looks that undress her, size her up in detail. She is embarrassed, uncomfortable, feels under attack. In a corner she notices Nayla engrossed in her writing. She has not seen her. Hayate does not wish to disturb her. She is sitting at a table with men and women debating current events in loud voices. Hayate approaches the group. Rima welcomes her with enthusiasm and introduces her:

'This is Hayate, from Lebanon, in exile among us this year, to inspire us, to bring us new ideas, that we might support the oppressed!'

11

And she bursts out laughing. Her mischievous eyes shine in her glasses, even at times of great fatigue such as she is now experiencing – Hayate would learn of this later. Hayate admires her eagerness to work and her eloquence. A well-known and appreciated journalist, she has a sense of humour rarely found among Arab women. She leans toward Hayate: 'We are waiting for Samia before ordering lunch.'

Hayate orders coffee, takes her cigarettes and passes them around the table. The others continue their discussion. The tone, the vehemence of their words remind Hayate of other places, other debates – a Beirut before the war. The same liveliness, the same well-turned phrases, the same revolt, the same speeches, different problems . . .

Suddenly a hand touches her arm. Nayla gives her some sheets of paper folded in four. Hayate opens them. They are covered with a tormented, feverish scrawl. Nayla urges her to fold them up again.

'Don't read them now. Hang on to them. For when you're alone.'

Hayate looks at her, moved by this act of confidence, by this sign of friendship. She folds them, slips them into her bag. She would like to hold Nayla back, but she has already turned towards the door.

'I have to go home. My mother is waiting for me. I promised to take her for a walk this afternoon.'

'I'll stop and see you tomorrow evening perhaps, when I return from Tunis.'

Nayla leaves with an air of sadness and a heavy step. Her brisk, nervous gestures, a certain abruptness in her words, her coarse, breaking voice, sometimes reflect her inner conflict, her search for a core, the very heart of existence. The day's problems disturb her. She dreams of a better and more equitable future, and thirsts with the desire to help others.

Samia, Rima and Hayate climb the streets of the Médina looking for a restaurant. The souk, animated and colourful, swells with people. The sun shimmers on the silks, woollens, copper, jewellery, glassware, wooden trinkets, pottery, rugs, mirrors, perfume and spices. The crowd undulates in the heat like an undying wave mounting towards the sky.

Rima knows the labyrinths of the Médina, having spent her childhood here. She leads the women along narrow alleys unknown to tourists, and even to some Tunisians. She speaks easily, happy to share her experience, to tell of her past with her body, her movements and her vision of the future. Her enthusiasm conveys optimism, and her hospitality is unending. Hayate feels privileged to share in this spontaneous expression of a woman's life, her sorrows and hopes.

Rima brings them to a restaurant filled with people, smoke, the smells of lamb and grilled fish, strong cumin and red peppers, olive oil and garlic. They have some difficulty finding seats around a table and encounter the surprised stares of men and of women chaperoned by men. Rima and Samia are not uncomfortable with these critical looks. They are used to asserting themselves in a society which does everything to exclude them, erase them, keep them silent. With their gracious walk, fluid movements and direct language, these women cut their own path, make a place for themselves in forbidden areas, affirm who they are, and that no one will displace them or send them back to the harem. They talk of places like the Médina with a certain nostalgia, but they distrust this past as if it were a labyrinth ready to close in upon them.

Rima orders the meal. For the past two days, Samia has been sheltering a cousin who has left her village and an abusive husband. Samia has contacted her journalist women friends; they will write her story to sway public opinion – the cheeks of her cousin still bear the marks of cigarette burns. Her husband had tied her to a chair to beat her, and had struck her in the stomach, even though she was several months pregnant. Her cousin does not want to keep the child for whom she fears a similar fate, and refuses to return to this brutal man. Samia, who has also suffered greatly, has sworn to help her to the bitter end, despite all obstacles; her own family accuses her of inciting her cousin to rebel.

Samia, somewhat distant and reserved with Hayate, tells this story with fire and passion. Malicious eyes gleam behind her glasses. In her hair, a pink and violet slide in the form of a butterfly gives her face a sly look. She continues, heatedly:

'I'm used to fighting! I'll do it for her too! We will not give up the struggle because certain men have decided to take away the few rights we have won! Like in Monastir three weeks ago . . .'

Rima interrupts, offering plates of savoury mechouïa, well-seasoned grilled meat, bread and glasses of lemonade.

'What happened in Monastir?' Hayate asks.

'There was a meeting with some Tunisian lawyers. They declared that Bourguiba had gone too far in his emancipation of women and that Tunisia must return to Islamic law, where answers to all the needs of women can be found. A delegation of women lawyers – with a man at their head! – objected that we could not and must not leave it to the past any longer to solve future problems. They were silenced with a reminder that the Koran had proclaimed that nothing good could come from a woman leader, that women are too emotional, do not have the intellectual capacity of men, or something like that! Do you realise how they're trying to make us live? In the Middle Ages, no less!'

Hayate listened intently. 'What are you going to do?' she asks.

'I won't stay if an oppressive regime comes to power,' Samia replies quickly.

'We'll fight,' says Rima. 'We won't allow repression to become established.'

Hayate gazes at them with admiration. These two women are

14

like embers igniting a fire of warmth, light, justice and love for transformation of the Arab world! Both burn with a contagious passion that visibly consumes them.

Rima reminds them of the Club meeting. They pay the bill and once again pass through the labyrinth of the Médina that Hayate is beginning to get to know. They go up and down, worming their way through alleyways. They turn down passages and come out at a square where boys are playing soccer, then take a passageway that ends at the Club. It is situated on the grounds of a former palace, with its domed rooms like cellars; the place is picturesque, with its past – stones that tell their story, walls in which voices resonate. This place is in keeping with the present, due to renovations, to the desire to make it the city's centre for cultural activities, right in the middle of the market district.

The meeting room is already full of women. One of them, a psychiatrist, explains an article which establishes the link between sexuality and identity. She refers to her own situation. The big question for her is the profound alienation, the contradiction that she has noticed between her sexual life and her professional life. She has never been able to combine the two in a harmonious way.

Other women take the floor. They express their uneasiness, their difficulties, the sexual problems they have encountered, and what these may signify for Tunisian society:

'Men are not secure and cannot reassure us. I don't dare ask anything of a man on a sexual level, but I refuse to be castrated in order to remain the little girl I was, the one they want me to be again.'

'The identity problem we face is determined by the sexual crisis we're going through.'

'For Tunisian women in general, sexuality still means reproduction. A man is traumatised by impotence whereas a woman agonises over infertility and not the lack of orgasm. In the past, women didn't ask such questions, now they do. My mother, when she climaxed, would say the next day: "I had an orgasm, I am a whore!"'

A woman psychiatrist takes up the discussion:

'The Arab male is afraid of the female orgasm, afraid of her bestiality, afraid she will be unfaithful to him. In a relationship, the man's stakes are higher than the woman's. For the man, a bad experience can drive him to a psychosis, whereas for a woman, it's neurosis. A psychosis is much more serious. Men are therefore very afraid, for in losing their sexual identity, they can lose everything. So they live with this anguish. If one understands that, one can see more clearly and better maintain a relationship. Despite my awareness of these fears, I've never been able to foster a good relationship. After many negative experiences, I finally told myself: I have the right to experience pleasure, but if orgasm entails dependency, masochism, an end to my development as an individual in my own right, then what am I to do? I prefer to renounce sexual pleasure if it means putting the brakes on my own growth. But that is a personal decision. It may not be right for others. One must be conscious of these dilemmas, and make an informed decision.'

Hayate thinks of a maid she had often spoken with, in a house she stayed in before her move to Salammbô. For her, the problem was above all material, financial. How could she live on fifty dinars a month and raise a sick daughter by herself having been abandoned by her husband? She had shown Hayate photos of her wedding where she was beautiful and slender; now she had gained a lot of weight and felt ugly. Hayate had noticed the sadness already in her eyes! Now the maid had but one goal: to leave the country, to find work elsewhere! This summed up Hayate's discussions with most of the domestic help she had met.

Hayate's thoughts then turned to Afafe, a young Arabic scholar preparing a thesis on literature. The previous week, she had eaten fish with Afafe at the seashore. There was in her, too, rebellion and bitterness mixed with an exuberant joy for living! She had told Hayate of her disastrous experiences with men, her search for love and absolutes, her disillusionment. Her suffering stemmed from not being able to separate sex and feelings because she gives her whole self, body and soul!

These women, these women
of Salammbô, of Sidi Bou Saïd,
of Tunis, Gafsa, Tozeur,
of Monastir, Carthage, Kaïrouan,
of Bizerte, Gabès, Métovia, Chot El Djerid,
of Kebili, Deguèche, Metaloui, La Marsa,
all these women,
each with scars in their words,
open wounds in their hearts,
tears in their writing,
cries in their song,
voices which call out, grow stronger, tear,
pierce the indifference of the sky,
light a thousand fires of rebellion and hope.

4

Aïda lives in a working class district of Tunis. The houses are one-storey, the streets dusty and poorly maintained. They remind Hayate of certain neighbourhoods, certain streets, the houses of adobe, the dust of Omdurmane in the Sudan where last year she had researched women's issues, in particular, the practice of infibulation. Inside, life is intense, and seeks an outlet, a force which the dust envelops in silence and loss.

Hayate goes into a shop to buy a few things: rice, vermicelli, butter, meat, vegetables and fruit. The storekeeper recognises her accent from the Mashrek and asks her if she is Palestinian. When she says that she is Lebanese, he expresses his regret about Lebanon, laments the war, rages against Zionism, Arab governments 'which do nothing' and politics in general. Hayate would have liked to buy a bottle of wine, but there was none to be had in this poor neighbourhood. She thanks him, pays and leaves.

Aïda's living room is full of women sitting everywhere. They talk loudly through a thick cloud of smoke. They want to create a publication for women, a magazine in which they would finally be able to express what torments them. In this way, they could make their voices heard, unveil and reveal society's ills.

The most pressing concern is financial: where can they obtain the funds to begin? They decide to refuse all help from institutions or individuals to whom they would be accountable; they do not want to see themselves limited in what they have to say by economic pressures, however friendly. They decide to chip in, even at the cost of enormous sacrifice. For some of them, fifty dinars is more than a quarter of their monthly salary. Even so, they give it whole-heartedly.

They organise themselves into committees assigned to cover different sections of the journal and try to find a name that will be easy to remember and present them in the best possible light. They want to avoid a hierarchical structure in order to ease communication. What each has to say, write, explain and analyse is important. No piece of writing or single voice should claim superiority over another. It is difficult to put such a lofty ideal into practice!

They are thirty or so women, striving for the success of this journal which lies outside the norm, outside masculine frameworks and existing models. What an enterprise! They invent, create their own models, their own organisation based on respect and recognition of one other. They choose a president, not the most eloquent or talented one, but the most well-liked, the one who will know how to reconcile differences, smooth the rough edges, promote acceptance through tolerance.

The cigarette smoke thickens. A single window is just half-opened so as not to attract the attention of neighbours. The discussions are animated, passionate! Enthusiasm lights their faces.

> To create a new journal
> With new ideas
> Far from dogma, authorities,
> From systems built on fear
> To bring it into the world as a child for the future
> Show the child the possibility of other relationships
> Based on respecting difference
> To converse with the other, him, her, every day
> To open the other to hope
> Rebirth of a better world of life and light!
> To give this child all the fruits of the earth,
> All the sap from the trees,
> All the seeds of the fields,
> So that a continent of wheat, of bread, of love
> May rise, climb, multiply!

Hayate feels a little out of place in this group of Tunisians. She slips out and goes to the kitchen to prepare the dish she promised. She sautés the vermicelli in butter and adds the rice, some salt, pepper and cups of boiling water. In another pan, she pours some olive oil, sautés the onions and garlic, then browns the meat, and finally adds the vegetables and tomato sauce, not forgetting to add more salt and pepper and above all cinnamon, the secret of Lebanese dishes. A delicious smell pervades the place.

Aïda's daughter, Saïda, arrives famished. Hayate gives her a piece of fruit and asks her to wait. Then she picks a corner in which to sit and write in her diary. She finds the pages Nayla has slipped into it, unfolds them and starts to read. She is immediately struck by the passionate, broken tone, the evocative and brutal images. It is a violent treatise against society, starting with her family, especially her father. The violence of certain passages reminds her of her first novel, which also denounces the hypocrisy of society and the role of her father.

During the course of her reading, she does not hear Halima come in.

'That smells so good! What are you doing sitting in the corner?'

'I'm making a dish I promised Aïda. I stayed for part of the meeting. I thought it was better to leave you to yourselves. There are things you need to discuss alone. It's good to see you. How are you?'

She watches Halima, pretty in her pale green outfit, her golden hair floating on her shoulders, her mouth a little sad and her gaze which fills with anguish when she thinks she is not being watched. Halima writes in Arabic, unusual for many women of her generation. On her own like Aïda, she works in an agency in order to earn a living, to raise her daughter. She is also a journalist and writes poetry. The women have asked her to edit the articles in Arabic; the journal will be bilingual. 'I've been very tired lately,' she sighs.

'There is too much to do; everything fires me up, so I exhaust myself trying to keep up with all of it. Apart from that, everything's fine. And how about you? You're living in Salammbô? What do you think about the meeting and the new journal?'

'I'm very impressed! It gives me hope for women and for the Arab world in general. There will be problems of course, but if

20

this project works out, it will lead to other possibilities we may not be aware of now. In any case, it's a great start, don't you think?'

Halima frowns: 'I see too many problems! But the project inspires me and I'm going to give it everything I've got.'

'What are the difficulties you foresee?'

'Several irreconcilable ideologies will bump heads. They are represented by women active in different parties and institutions who support the interests of their establishment. Disputes are inevitable.'

'The aim of forming the group, and the founding of a publication for women is precisely that – to go beyond these quarrels which take up men's discourse and undermine women's issues.'

'I hope so, but I'm sceptical. I've seen too many fierce differences and groups splitting up to believe in the possibility of union.'

'You know Fanon's thesis: the oppressed fight among themselves and play the game of the oppressor. Let's not accept that analysis as inevitable. Let's work to rise above it, to create new relationships.'

'I'd like to, but I'm still a non-believer. We'll talk about it another time if you like; right now I've got to go home.'

'When are you coming to visit, you and your daughter? I'm in a beautiful spot at the edge of the sea. Come for the weekend.'

'I'd love to. Do you have a telephone?'

'Yes, I'll give you the number. Don't you want to stay for a taste of my Lebanese cooking?'

'I'd love to, but I still have to help my daughter with her homework, and I'm really tired. Another time, perhaps.'

Hayate scribbles her phone number on a scrap of paper and they give each other a hug. Halima leaves and Hayate continues reading Nayla's writing, which begins with: 'My sister who troubles me, also touches me.' The more she reads, the more she is stirred by the emotion it arouses:

'I deliver here a few bits and pieces of my torn and scattered self, which has never known unity. You want me to weave a

21

cloth of suffering and hope with these scraps . . . I am
working at it, not without pain, but also with much hope!
. . . To speak about one's own experience is a sort of
personal death ceremonial . . . The cry of Leïla Baalbakki: "I
live!" and the resonance of the Arab words "*ana ahya*"! have
awakened in me sensations, passions long repressed in the
depths of my being . . . I've lived my life smothering myself
in order not to live any longer.'

Hayate wanted to copy down all of these pages into her own
diary. Her words are so beautiful! But out of respect for Nayla's
trust in her, she hides these pages which would tear down walls,
which would reveal the inner centre of discovery, a revelation of
the self and others, a place of understanding and communication!
Nayla must be the one to speak out, to assume the responsibility
of opening herself to others. She must be the one to communicate
her experience, then others will also understand this process which
transforms life, which brings to the forefront the foundations of
the world's lies.

Touched by her reading, Hayate jots down these few lines:

'Nayal, Nayla, my sister! Your pages have moved me. It's
hard to express everything I felt reading your words – there
was so much beauty, such brute force and also moving
sensitivity in your writing. You write so well! I did well to
encourage you to put your thoughts on paper! And you
knew it! You are afraid . . . and with good reason. One is
always afraid to encounter the force of a passion that (as you
know) is going to devour you, take hold of you and cause
you to live differently at a level of truth that few others ever
attain. I don't believe that this will create a mask, a double
life, and restrict you from being yourself. No, on the
contrary, writing will help you to live a fuller life.

'You communicate so well – your life, your past, your
solitude, your rebellion, your aspirations. So much violence
and anguish, as if you were tearing bits of flesh from all of

the scars of your life. Themes and questions meet, cross each other, come and go: speech, writing . . . Your mother who won't speak any more because she has already given too much, your father who speaks too much because he is afraid of the silence created by your mother; speech interrupted . . . and what of you in all this? You walk and you walk in the city, in search of truth, of justice. You move around in the stifling space of your house, which has smothered you since childhood, prevented you from writing, from blossoming . . . your father slamming the doors, the lost gaze of your mother, the looks, the looks . . . a returning theme, expressed like no other . . . fleeing and penetrating eyes, the unbounded gaze of your mother . . . the violence of slamming doors, the aggression of the city, doors closed in the face of young people, sealed lips, atrophied youth . . . and you, in search of yourself, expressing in words your sensations, a growing, climbing voice, becoming a melodious song, calming and full of sorrow. If only you knew how well I understand what you have lived through and how happy I am you are writing! Write, write!'

> Wild flower crushed by the gunfire
> Of my crazed country
> I gather you
> Dust in the hollow of my hand
> I water you with the tears of my wound
> I blow across your wound a song of hope
> I give your roots the waters of happiness
> For your petals to open
> In brilliant blossoms like the palette of the rainbow
> For your stem to reach toward the star of healing
> For you to find a creative serenity
> For the shepherd to find peace again
> Far from the anger of snipers
> Rapists, killers of hope,
> For the mountain to burst

With the hymn of grasshoppers
Announcing the return to life.

With the meeting over, some of the women leave, others stay to share the meal, to talk and tell of their life experiences, their desires, dreams. The kitchen is full. Hayate serves; Aïda opens the windows of the living room to freshen the air. The wind enters in strong gusts – a storm is in the making. Rima, who had disappeared for a moment, returns loaded down with a box full of honey and almond cakes. Hayate was just wondering if there would be enough to eat. But this is the kind of question that is never asked in Tunis and in the Arab world: there is always enough for everyone! What one has, one shares readily. So why are the civil wars so violent? Why this need to defend territory and possessions with a feeling of honour which is nourished by the fantasy of protecting the women, when one can be so generous when it comes to hospitality? Is it the sexuality and procreative power of women which provokes fear and carries with it division and the unleashing of hate and love? Is it really the relationship to women that stirs up all this passion? Or is it that customs of hospitality are outside the rites of honour bound up with sexuality, for they do not threaten the structure of the clan? Or can it be the complexity that lies in the contradiction of feelings when it is a question of the gift and the exchange? Are these questions valid for the women of the group who have different values and who try to live differently?

The women make compliments about the Lebanese dish. Hayate loves the Tunisian cakes. Everyone eats their fill and Aïda makes herbal tea. It is midnight before all the women have gone. Rain beats against the window panes and the doors are rattled by the storm. Aïda lights a candle which flickers – she needs to talk. She pours another cup of vervain for Hayate who is sitting on the rug. They lie back against the cushions, smoke in silence. Aïda comes out of a long and painful daydream:

'My first love was a stranger to this country. He brought me a breath of freedom and an appreciation of things I had never

24

known. We are still good friends, and I often visit him and the wife he married later. I was afraid to live my life with him – I didn't want to hurt my father, to live far from him, even though he had always encouraged me to be myself. And back then so many things were happening in Tunisia. I returned home and married a left-wing Tunisian man. I thought that together we would take part in our society's revolution, or at least help change certain things, starting with our own relationship. What happened was that (and I couldn't have predicted it) like many left-wing men, my husband entertained revolutionary ideas on the level of politics, but in his personal life he remained conservative and traditional. This was something I discovered early on and it was very hard to accept. I hope that my daughter's generation will benefit from our experiences and won't make the same mistakes.'

Aïda sighs and has difficulty continuing. The storm's harsh beating accompanies her trembling. She begins again in a tearful voice:

'When my second child was born – the first died and I had trouble recovering from that – I felt abandoned. I had no experience with babies and no one to ask. I found myself alone, helpless, unhappy. This was not at all how I had imagined marriage, and I couldn't stand being shut in all day long with no link with the outside world. It was a difficult period. He didn't like the way I kept house; he found it deplorable. It's true, I don't enjoy household chores – and even less so back then – I prefer investing my energy in more stimulating activities. My husband had been seeing a woman friend of mine for a long time. I was naive – I didn't suspect anything. It's something I could never have done to a friend of mine! One day, he announced that he was going to live with her. I let him go. In a way, it was a relief. We never got along, either on a physical level or in an emotional or psychological sense. Still, I felt alone and distraught. We divorced. I was able to get through this trial with the help of the women's group which was forming. We had all experienced similar things: leftist ideas which had taken little effect in our private lives. Fortunately, there was the group; we could talk about our disillusionment and try to

25

overcome the suffering. I was very discouraged. I decided to work as a schoolteacher and to take up journalism again in order to expose the ills of our society. I didn't know what was ahead for me . . .'

Her voice breaks. She is gripped with sobs and cannot go on. Hayate comes closer and consoles her, massaging her knotted neck. Aïda smiles in the midst of her tears: 'It feels good to cry and to talk. Your fingers on my neck are undoing my suffering. This rain has a calming effect and takes away my tiredness. The disappointments of my personal life were nothing compared to what was waiting for me in the social arena when I tried to speak, to cry out, to write about the injustices I had seen, that I was studying and which disgusted me. I was arrested, imprisoned for my audacity . . . tortured . . . Does it shock you that this happens in the country one calls the most democratic in the Arab world?'

'Yes, it's shocking to me, and at the same time, it's not . . . we are living through difficult times in our society. Sometimes I feel so bad about what's happening, especially in my own country, Lebanon, that I wish I had been born somewhere else, in another area of the world. I can't turn my back on my country even if it tears me apart; I am too involved. Your story is unsettling and I understand you so well. I rebelled against the injustice and oppression of my society as well. I didn't have the courage to face them as you have. It was not until later, after having left and established myself elsewhere, that I could take part in concrete actions, such as the teaching of subjects related to the problems in our societies. And I became aware that our dilemmas were not so different from those of other societies in the world. More and more, my view of the world allows me to identify problems better and work out the most effective solutions. I can teach the literature of the Mashrek and the Maghreb in all countries where it has been translated. I put myself into writing, into song, and I return home when possible, because there I can make a direct impact like you. Your life is an inspiration to me!'

Hayate's eyes shine as she speaks. The two women sitting on cushions look upon each other with admiration, their radiant faces

26

illuminated by candlelight. They are turned towards the future and projects full of hope. Their friendship will carry them far, will give them the strength to continue. Outside, the storm has calmed down. The doors and blinds no longer rattle. The rain is but a soft murmur fading away.

5

Hayate boards the train for Salammbô. There are fewer people this time; it is not rush hour. She finds a seat and admires the countryside rolling by. It is a clear morning, washed by the night's storm. Flat, still lagoon, purified by rain, lights placed there like mirrors; the smell of stagnant water stirred up by the shower, the smell of sea and seaweed. She breathes deeply and smiles, thinking of Aïda and their deepening friendship. Yesterday, she was saddened by the tragedy of being born in this part of the world where so much violence is unleashed. Today, she tells herself, what a joy to know such marvellous people, and in this part of the world, like metals rendered more precious by exposure to flame! What a joy, too, to be born in this time when women are becoming much more aware!

She takes a book from her bag, *La Citadelle d'Osta*, borrowed from Nayla. She is struck by the power of certain passages:

And Maryam? Maryam like millions of others, saw blue colour the window panes of her country, and for the first time. She was the victim of wild insanity, for Maryam was thinking of a time when war was linked with truth. She thought that authenticity was absolutely unattainable, religious faith a crazy impossibility and that all absolutes were nothing short of impossible. The human being felt all of this within himself, saw the image of a hero who offered his soul as the price of the land. It had taken only a few years for heroism to become tainted. And for the myth to die. And with each new martyr, countries distance themselves from the land, one after another . . . One day, at some point in his life, every human being must know the transparency of the dream. He must live the absolute, erase the vast contradiction between ideas and their realisation, even at the cost of his own life, at the cost of his household . . . even at the price of the blood of Osta, the innocent one. And me? I was passing from endurance to wandering. And I discovered that nothing could shock me any more. I would no longer listen to words spoken as if they were the truth. They were dead and the element of surprise had died in me. It had disappeared, just like that. Just as the heroics of heroes had passed away.

Hayate sighs, closes the book. Was this the meaning of war? Thirst for truth and absolutes, the need to erase contradictions? To believe in heroes and then to stop believing? These words frighten her. How could one ever believe war to be a solution? Don't people learn anything from history? Understanding and accepting contradictions, are these not the beginning of maturity, the path toward tolerance? The recognition of difference, a plurality of ideas, reflection through dialogue, is that not the salvation of humanity? Why not seek out the absolutes of life through the subtleties and complexities of existence rather than by making war for a so-called faith in an Absolute?

She panics, envisaging war, the chasm of death and violence, the unfurling of an interminable hatred. She agonises over the thought of her sister and brother there, the bombings; perhaps they are in shelters even now. But her brother's house has no shelter. She fears for him and his family. She will try to call him from the house.

The train has already arrived, standing before the quaint railway station in Salammbô. On the platform, she is entranced by the air's luminosity; it appears to reverberate with the brilliance of a sea as yet distant, but which sends out reflections from its mirrored surface. She takes the main road and arrives at Nayla's house. She slips the letter from the day before through the door. On the envelope, she writes: 'To Nayla, my sister and friend.'

She hurries back to the house, to place a call to Lebanon. She stops in a little shop to buy some cheese and bread and returns along the beach; the sea is shining. Washed by rain, caressed by wind, it glints and sparkles. She approaches her house and is surprised by the open gate. The owner is in the garden about to leave: 'I brought you the lamp you asked for. Do you need anything else?'

'You were to bring in a larger bed. The one inside is much too narrow.'

He looks her over from head to toe, as if her request were indecent. His gaze is obscene, charged with unspoken meaning.

'You live alone, don't you? Why do you need a bigger bed?' he slowly asks.

His remark angers her.

'The bed is very uncomfortable,' she throws back. 'And my private life is none of your business!'

She should not have made this type of remark. She must keep calm, at all costs! In a country where women are considered permanently under age, at the mercy of male authority, she should not have shown her irritation. The owner reddens and retorts:

'I'm sorry, but I have no other bed. You can leave if you don't like it here.'

He knows very well that she is at his mercy; she has paid two months rent up front and has no recourse; her friends are themselves facing difficulties much more serious. She turns her back on him and crosses the garden. She feels his eyes studying her. She is happy when she's finally able to go inside and lock the door – a false sense of security! Why did he go in when she wasn't at home? Does he have the right to do so? She must find out.

She is trembling with annoyance. The landlord is certainly a very unpleasant man. In the beginning, if she had not dealt with his wife, perhaps she would not have rented this house despite its advantages: the proximity of the sea, the courtyard for meals and even meetings, a bright kitchen overlooking the sea, the space to work, hot water, a telephone . . .

She makes a cup of coffee and hurries to the phone. She dials the operator.

'Beirut, please. The number . . .'

'Beirut is very difficult to reach, Madame, but we will try.'

'Please, you must get through. My sister is there, under threat of bombings.'

The operator sympathises: 'Yes, Madame, we will attempt the impossible. We'll call you when we get through.'

She hears a knock at the door, runs to it and sees Nayla, with her large and somewhat awkward smile. She asks to come inside.

'Why have you closed your doors and windows? It's so nice outside today.'

'Yes, I know, but I've just returned. I'm trying to reach Lebanon.'

She doesn't want to upset Nayla with stories about the landlord when they have so many other things to discuss.

'I'll make a cup of coffee.'

'No, no, I don't want anything! Let's have a cigarette on the patio.'

She appears nervous and overexcited as she lights up. Holding out a packet to Hayate, she speaks rapidly:

'We didn't obtain permission to write the report on women who work in the local factory. The authorities are afraid. We should have expected it – it's not the first time they've refused me authorisation. I once went against them and I almost paid the price of my freedom. I'm not afraid. I'd do it again.'

'Would you like me to ask permission? I could say that it's part of my research.'

'No, it won't work. And now they're suspicious. For you, as a foreigner, it would be even worse. They're trying to hide things they certainly wouldn't want foreigners to see! I'm convinced that the working conditions of these women must be deplorable. It disgusts me! How can we make the abuses known before it's too late?'

'Couldn't you do an article, write that you've been refused authorisation?'

'Yes, and say what? It's not the first time I've been refused. It's become so frequent that no one is surprised by it any more. No,

31

no, forget what I've said; in any case, I have a thousand other things to finish.'

'Yes, I know, you wanted to talk to me about your thesis, didn't you?'

'My study of Nathalie Sarraute? Now I think that she doesn't make much sense. I would be better off writing about North African novelists. Your arrival made me see the importance, the beauty of this literature, but there's no specialisation in that subject here at the university. Does that surprise you?'

'Yes and no; it's the same in Lebanon. If I had stayed there, I would never have been able to specialise in and teach Black African, North African and Middle Eastern Studies. It's the colonial heritage. We are rid of it politically, perhaps, but not culturally, nor psychologically. At the moment, we're not able to promote our values, to recognise the beauty of our own culture. Those who assert themselves do so by *reaction* to the West and not through *self-affirmation*, and this brings about violence, fanaticism and a return to traditions and outdated value systems.'

'All this wears me out! ... How can I or anyone specialise in North African literature here within the Maghreb? It's absurd. I chose Nathalie Sarraute because I have a marvellous professor – a French woman I admire enormously and who understands me very well.'

'I was influenced by an extraordinary professor, too. I would not be where I am today without him. I understand your weariness and distress. That North African literature is not offered as an area of specialisation in North African universities is appalling. It's up to us to change things. It will take some time and perseverance.'

Because of Nayla's state of mind, Hayate should not have added:

'You see, America *can* bring about good things. Thanks to the black revolutionary movements, to the grass roots and women's movements, we have departments and programs offering subjects considered marginal in the past. I couldn't teach and obtain research grants for subjects so dear to us in any other country.'

'But it's a country with the means!' Nayla exclaims impatiently. 'It buys us with its dollars, with its economic power that devours us. Our culture and literature – it gathers it in, making a sweet sauce filled with hormones and other chemical additives. Oh! I'm so sick of it! This conversation is giving me a headache. I must go to work. Give me your novel about Lebanon to read, the pages you've already written.'

Hayate would love to find some words to soothe Nayla and help her to find the way which would allow her to blossom. She goes to her cupboard and brings back a book and a file: 'Here, I'll give you a short story about my sister, written several years ago. You already have my first novel. Here are a few pages of the second I'm working on. I'd like to hear your comments. When you have some time, perhaps we could also talk about the articles and books you've lent me.'

Nayla leaves as she had come, the fleeting passage of a wounded star.

Hayate goes to her desk and opens her diary. Later, she will have to reconstruct these emotions, these faces, these smells, the flat and immobile lagoon which links the city to the surrounding suburb and to the sea, this sea that never ceases to astonish her with its abrupt and varied changes. Now, it is black and tensing for the approaching storm.

> What can one do in the face of deprivation?
> No time,
> No money,
> No place of one's own,
> No practical means of transport,
> No blossoming, loving sexuality,
> No opportunities,
> But missed chances?
> Fear and anguish of seeing the little one owns
> taken away.

In the middle of the evening, the telephone rings. It is the operator: 'I'm sorry, Madame, Beirut . . . is impossible to reach.'

33

'Thank you for trying.'

She hangs up, goes to bed.

Beirut impossible, impossible . . .

She falls asleep in tears.

She is wakened by the telephone again. An operator announces: 'Madame, it's Paris.'

'Hello, darling, did I wake you? Forgive me. I've been trying to get through for a while.'

'I've tried to get through to Beirut, but it's impossible they tell me. I'm so happy to hear from you. When are you coming over?'

'I don't know yet; I have a lot of work at the moment. What have you been doing? What's new?'

'It's too long to explain at such a distance; so much is happening.'

'Have you met some of the women from the Tunisian feminist movement?'

'I've met several. You were right – this movement is alive and active. I wish you could be here. You should come.'

'I will try. I miss you.'

'I miss you too.'

'We're going to be cut off. I'll call again. I love you.'

With a click, the telephone is cut by a machine looking for more coins. Hayate feels frustrated. These calls from so far away are exasperating – one hardly has time to say more than a few words. She feels terribly alone and upset in her little house by the sea, a sea mounting in a wind blowing ever stronger. All of a sudden she panics. She needs to hear the voice of a friend. She calls Aïda.

'I hope I didn't wake you. I need to talk to you.'

'Me too, I wanted to talk to you. What's going on? You sound upset.'

She tells her everything: the landlord, Nayla, the telephone calls, Beirut, Paris. She talks and talks, unloading her heavy heart. And she hears comforting words:

'That's a lot to handle in so few hours. This story about the landlord is appalling. At times like that, I understand violence. Unfortunately, as women, we haven't been taught how to defend

34

ourselves. We have to be aggressive with men like that, and not put up with it. We should take judo and karate lessons. In order to fight facism, I'm ready to grab a gun!'

Aïda's violent declaration makes Hayate laugh. It is a nervous laugh she is unable to control. All the afternoon's tension evaporates in the laughter. Aïda joins her.

'I'm so happy to hear you laugh! Let me tell you that I also spent an exasperating evening with my friend. He made me so nervous, I sent him home. I can't tolerate it when he's drunk. I'm looking for good communication with a man who will try to understand my expressions of tenderness. I like to drink wine from time to time, to be happy, open, relaxed, to enjoy life, but not to get myself drunk like him. And also, I have to get up early tomorrow to teach.'

'I'll let you sleep, dear friend. Thank you for listening. I'm so much calmer now.'

'You go to bed too. Don't think about this any more. We'll have coffee at the International Café tomorrow at midday if you like. And you can come and spend the weekend with me.'

'Or you can come here if you like. Good night.'

They hang up. She is at peace despite the storm rumbling in the distance. She could never point a gun. All weapons make her ill. Who invented those machines of death? And aggression makes her turn inward instead of reacting with violence. But speaking with Aïda has calmed her. She falls asleep and dreams.

A storm is unleashing itself upon the sea. Hayate dreams of her country floundering in insanity, murder and vengeance. She is on a boat tossed about by the wind; the high waves hold it down, keep it from moving forward. It turns around itself, dragged in a frenetic whirlwind; it is impossible for it to arrive at the harbour, to get beyond the fury and force of the hurricane. Suddenly, she is conscious of more than this cyclone of nature; bombs rain down upon the fragile shell of this sinking boat. She is very afraid, aware of death close at hand. She notices a beautiful bird flying overhead. She calls to it and holds out her arms. The bird descends and makes a cradle with its wings. She desperately clutches its strong neck, slides down and makes herself light upon the rug of its rainbow-coloured feathers. She lets herself be flown far from the shipwreck. She sings with the bird which ascends toward the crest of a mountain eternally covered in snow.

6

It's Saturday, meeting day at the Club Taher Haddad. Hayate rises early. This she does with pleasure when the sun shines and the sea sparkles. Sitting under the trees with a cup of *café au lait* and apricot jam spread on toast, she writes in her diary. She has not seen Nayla since her visit the other day. She glimpsed her once at the International Café. She seemed distant, preoccupied and anxious. In the middle of the week she had lunch in the Médina with Halima, who showed her the Institute of Arab Literature. She was impressed by the ease with which Halima entered a restaurant in the souks, filled exclusively with men. It was a rainy day; people in the market place seemed out of sorts. Everything was humid and wet. Halima had ordered Tunisian dishes – an appetiser of fried eggs on a bed of fried peppers and tomatoes, served with fried potatoes, everything swimming in oil. This was a rather heavy starter, but appropriate in the cold weather, with a delicious main course of grilled fish. They ate heartily and finished the meal with mint tea served in a Moorish café covered in mosaics, decorated with arabesques and Persian rugs. Halima had told her life story – the death of her husband, her feelings of liberation and guilt. She hesitated to speak, enclosed in a heart-ache, difficult to define, wanting to liberate herself yet being afraid to express it, dignified, poised, nervous as a wounded bird. They walked a long time in the rain, talking of work-related projects, contacts, visits. Hayate had returned home entranced, her heart filled with images, scents, colours, emotions.

She had seen Aïda several times with her daughter or her Palestinian friend, but most of the time alone. They had coffee together at the International Café and tea in the souks and they had talked and talked. They never tired of these long conversations in which they could open their hearts without fear, without holding back, confident that the other would understand, that they could tell each other anything. They felt supported by this friendship that had just begun, yet was already on solid ground. There are people with whom one knows instantly the relationship will be very strong and beautiful, she thinks. She had several friendships like this across the world on which she was able to rely. These marvellous, enriching people lifted her above life's bitter disappointments. 'I'm so happy to have made such a contact here, when I'm homesick for Lebanon,' she writes.

She puts away her diary, assembles some things that she puts into a bag, locks the house and walks down the road. She passes in front of Nayla's house, calls out to her. Nayla appears at the window in a nightshirt and motions for her to come upstairs. Happy about the welcome, Hayate climbs up the stairs quickly. Nayla is smiling and exuberant, as she is on good days. Her mother spent a restful night. She offers her a cup of coffee.

'Aren't you up early for a Saturday!'

'Early? It's already ten o'clock. When the sun shines like today, I don't have any trouble getting out of bed. What have you done this week?'

'Always the same old thing: teach, study, take care of my mother, read, write my thesis ... One important thing, I campaigned in a union meeting. I really think that the feminist movement has to associate itself with the left if it doesn't want to be marginalised.'

'I'm not sure I agree. It's often leftist movements that marginalise women – give them secondary roles in the organisations, use them when they need them, never make their agenda a priority or even of equal importance in debates.'

'You're wrong, Hay, read the book I gave you, *Féminisme et Marxisme*; you'll understand what I mean. By the way, can you return it soon? I'd like to use it to respond to what you've written about Lebanon. I don't agree with your argument. It's not sexuality that has caused the Lebanese crisis, it's politics.'

'But private life *is* political, isn't it? I wanted to expose an aspect of the debate that's often hidden. I don't claim that it's the whole

38

truth. It's a facet of the Lebanese conflict that one must not ignore. In fact, I wanted to ask you: could we organise a march for peace in Lebanon, like the one I was in last year in Beirut? A young woman at the institute where I was teaching decided one morning that she'd seen enough war, that the only solution was to reunite West Beirut with East Beirut and to march for peace along the line of demarcation, the point of rupture and separation. It was a magnificent initiative which should have brought together all the different civil communities of Lebanon to shout: "No to war! Yes to peace!"'

'You say "should have". Didn't this march take place?'

'Unfortunately not. "Blind" bombings which caused hundreds of deaths and injuries didn't allow it to happen. But the idea lives in people's hearts and will be taken up again. It must grow here and in other countries to ensure lasting peace.'

'I agree and I'd like to help you. We must begin by discussing it among us, in the Club and in the unions.'

'And with other people we know. Are you coming to the Club this afternoon?'

'I'm not sure yet. I have to take my mother out for a walk. She's been inside all week.'

Hayate stands up.

'I'll be going now. I'm meeting Rima and some others at the International Café. The book by Osseirane that you lent me is really beautiful. Her idea of war is both fascinating and frightening.'

'It's her personal experience, I think. She's been politically active in the Palestinian cause, from what I understood.'

'Who didn't side with the Palestinians at the beginning of the war? And who was not disillusioned?'

'Could you return that book, too? I don't remember it well. I'd like to reread it.'

'I'll bring you everything I've finished some time before the end of next week – or you could stop by my place one of these days.'

Hayate goes into the adjoining room to say hello to Nayla's mother who appears to recognise her and smiles. This smile means that she has spent a peaceful night. Nayla is happy with her mother's improvement. Once again, Hayate is touched by Nayla's tenderness and devotion. She leaves quickly to hide her strong emotions.

At the train station, she buys a newspaper and boards the train. Things must be better in Lebanon! No news is good news! There is not much in the paper, apart from Bourguiba's trips and visits from Mzali.

Hayate looks at the countryside. The sea is smooth and blue, turning to several shades of green. Clouds of birds stretch across the sky, widen and shrink back, like patterns of lace, disappearing to return in other harmonious forms – shapes of leaves, butterflies. It looks like my dreams, thinks Hayate; there are always birds, emblems of freedom, transcendence, love.

Rima and Aïda are waiting for her at the International Café. They are with some other women and appear quite excited about something. Aïda announces good news: they have obtained authorisation to begin publication of the journal. They hope to go to press the following month with the first issue. Rima explains how they will have a base in the Médina, a place for meetings, somewhere to receive and send mail and to stock the issues.

'I'll show it to you if you like. It's close to where I was born and spent my childhood.'

'Let's go,' says Aïda. 'I'd like to see it too.'

They climb the streets of the Médina, happy about this news, boosted by the thought of starting the journal and hopeful about the future. This vision illuminating them is accentuated by the strong midday sun. Most of the people are napping at this hour. They stop to drink freshly squeezed orange juice, then continue through narrow streets flooded with sunlight.

In this heat, among these smells of squeezed lemons and oranges, of honey, cumin and incense, at the end of an alley strewn with gold, rose petals, carpeted with jasmine and bougainvillaea, in the heart of this densely populated neighbourhood, in this atmosphere of springtime and renewal, appears Ahlame. Her black hair is glossy and curly and her mischievous hazel eyes twinkle with joy

40

and intelligence. Dressed in a great flowered skirt, a close-fitting black blouse and long earrings in the form of suns and birds, she holds out her hand warmly. Her words are colourful and elaborate, dramatic, emphatic and grandiose:

'I've wanted to meet you for a long time. What a unique occasion this is, in the place of our blossoming. The birth of feminism takes place here in a setting laden with tradition.'

'You have come to see the place,' exclaims Rima.

'Yes, if you like, but especially to meet her, the goddess of the world.'

And she points her finger towards Hayate who is fascinated by this enthusiastic reception.

'Rather, it's *you* who is the goddess of this place,' she replies to this warm greeting.

> A click of recognition
> the meeting hour is sounded
> (s)he is there, hand outstretched
> palm open
> fingers that gather the dew
> gift of sharing
> There are boats for the voyage
> multiple sensitivities gliding
> over open vocations
> In the night of wandering,
> velvet petals cling to the trees
> and speak of a day when all was possible

They have arrived. Rima eagerly opens the door. They enter the premises which resemble a cellar – round walls, a floor of beaten earth, heavy tables and wooden benches.

'A good sweep, some posters on the walls, shelves for magazines and books, and we'll make the place ours – our space where ideas, texts, meditations, theories will all germinate,' begins Rima. She is proud of her find and of the help of her family which comes from this neighbourhood.

41

'In the meantime, I'll order pastries and mint tea to celebrate the moment.'

'Good idea,' exclaims Aïda. 'I'm starving.'

Ahlame approaches Hayate:

'I'd like to read your novel. Where can I find it?'

'I'll give you a copy.'

'I'd love you to attend a sketch at the Club next week. I wrote it, and I'm performing it.'

'What you do is so beautiful, so intense,' affirms Aïda. 'We'll all be there.'

'It's very different from last year; that was weak by comparison. This time I dare to say it all. You see, I was criticised a lot for last year's performance, even by feminist friends; imagine what it will be like this year!'

'Yes, I can just imagine it. You're right. Surprise us all with your revelations about our problems. We need it. Shake up our lethargy and the narrow-minded ideas we have despite our declared feminism. Don't be afraid to say everything!'

'But I am afraid. Inside, I feel very vulnerable. I'm afraid of being criticised and hurt again. I look strong, but I'm really sensitive and fragile – if you only knew how much!'

Hayate places a hand on her shoulder.

'We're all like that. Or rather *I'm* like that too. Listening to you speak, I have the impression I'm hearing myself talk. We will be there to support you. So have no fear!'

Ahlame is very touched:

'I was right to want to meet you. My instinct rarely fails me. It's the most beautiful day of my life!'

Hayate is carried away by Ahlame's enthusiasm. She's thrilled about seeing the sketch. In her way of speaking there is a kind of exhilaration, a lyrical frenzy which she expresses by creating something which is out of the ordinary. Hayate has confidence in Aïda's assessment of her ability. She is seduced by the charm of these women with such provocative talent.

Rima serves warm crusty beignets, dusted with fine sugar and spilling with honey. The waiter from a nearby café brings sweet mint tea in little glasses decorated with flowers and a gold rim. The sugar and the tea renew their energy that the sun and the walk had exhausted.

'We're ready to return to the Club,' announces Rima, radiating with happiness.

◆

Today, each one speaks of how she came to feminism. Zahra takes the floor first:

'For me, feminism is a personal and political response to my situation and my relationship with power. I come from a conservative rural background. My father works in a factory. I am the eldest of seven children. For a very long time, my studies were the only thing that mattered in my life; school meant freedom. Where I come from, the relationship between men and women is very conventional. But I realised that at the University, it was the same. Women could not imagine themselves alone, and to destroy a woman, one often uses her private life. For a long time, I refused to go out with a militant. For me, living the life of a militant feminist would mean refusing all of the family pressure regarding marriage. I did not come to the Club to resolve my problems; I don't expect that from anyone. But different ideas expressed in the Club have helped me a lot. Feminists have a different relationship to politics. Feminism has helped me to establish my identity and to be independent. Because of my new confidence in myself, I can now confront politics without letting myself be dominated.'

'I was also born in a small village,' Samia continues, 'where women are very oppressed. Very early in life, I was told that girls who were not virgins were killed. I was lucky to have a mother from outside the village; she had studied in Tunis. When she was fourteen, her brother decided to marry her to her uncle. She was moved to this very traditional village. Her husband, my father, shut her in and beat her. She had her first child at the age of sixteen, then two more at eighteen. She became severely depressed. Early on, I learned of my mother's trials and I swore that I would not live like her. I learned to demystify the world of men at a very young age. I told my mother I didn't want to marry: I wanted to study. Some of my illiterate cousins had died under the blows of husbands and I said that I would never accept that fate. But, in one sense, I did the opposite of what I wanted. I was living an ambiguous lifestyle – I married at the age of twenty-two. I wanted a divorce immediately because from the beginning, it didn't work. However, I stayed married ten years! That blocked me intellectually and kept me from finishing my studies. I divorced, and took up my studies and research again. I always saw the socio-economic element as the most determining factor. I had never joined a political group – my route was individual. I began to prepare a study of sexism in education, specifically among schoolteachers. Then I discovered the Club. Since then, I no longer feel marginal and alone. I realised that my experience resembled that of other women. At the Club, I found enriching friendships. Before, I couldn't handle the solitude, now I live happily like that. If I had found the Club earlier, I wouldn't have waited ten years for my divorce!'

'I don't remember my childhood well,' Dalale says next. 'I think that I've always been a feminist. There are ways of behaving I have never accepted from men or women. The day I resolved the question of God, I began to live. Religion prevented me from moving forward. I told myself that if I had been able to stand up to that power, I should be able to rid myself of others. That gave me immense strength which enabled me to confront authority at the university. I have never been able to adhere to a political party. One day, a woman dragged me to the Club, and there I saw myself blossom. After God, it was the Club! Feminism, for me, is a societal project. It is another vision of things. I'd like to work for the liberation of the entire society, for if we free women, men will also be free.'

Halima speaks last:

'I have never had an easy relationship with my mother. She was an illiterate woman but intelligent; she should have studied. Instead, she encouraged me to study in her place. At the same time, she was very authoritarian and made all the decisions without consulting me. My father was also very strict – he forbade me to go out – but it was possible to discuss things with him. I got tired of my parents' supervision. I would have liked to leave the country to study or marry an intelligent man in order to be free. I didn't have the financial means to leave the country, so I married. I continued my studies within the marriage. Problems arrived when I had my daughter; I had too much work and no help. During the first years, it was as if I were illiterate. I didn't read anything. I didn't do anything. I felt cut off from everything, from all that made me happy. I realised that marriage is a prison; marriage makes you a child, and puts you socially on the side of women who stay at home, take care of children, and do nothing in the outside world. It gave me an image of myself I didn't like. I wondered why men sell women short; that's what brought me to feminism. I had sworn not to be like women who complain, but when I had my daughter, I saw myself repeating everything I had hated in my mother. Then I had serious problems with my husband. We no longer had anything to say to one another. Daily life together had destroyed the aspect of discovery. I had thought that marriage would allow me to resolve many personal and political problems, but when my daughter was born, talking with my husband became impossible. When he died, we were in a state of crisis.'

Halima bursts into tears. The women come forward to console her. Some of them ask her to continue. She does so, between sobs:

'It was hard to take on the responsibility of raising my daughter alone and to deal with my husband's death. My family helped me a lot. It is then that I came to the Club. That allowed me to get out. I joined a musical group as well. I organised myself. I devoured everything written by Simone de Beauvoir. I realised the serious nature of women's problems. Feminism is a way of seeing, of being, of exchanging. At the Club I learned to reflect with others. That has stimulated my ideas a lot.'

Halima begins to cry again. Others surround her, comfort her. They go to a corner of the room where Halima can let her tears flow freely. It is marvellously cathartic to express one's pain and past suffering in the presence of other women who are also wounded inside.

> The unfurling sweetness of confiding
> Welcoming circle of communication
> Women's hands outstretched, open
> link affection to sharing,
> wounds to speech,
> suffering to exchange
> The past is unwoven and life rewoven
> Masks are erased with healing oil
> Faces light up with the elixir of words
> Shoulders straighten under the balm of sympathy
> A procession of friendship dances
> to understand, console, dress the wounds
> and to express the joy of creation
> In a winter of waiting, a place calls out
> and says
> Heart of the Médina
> Centre of upheaval
> Place of renewal
> Place of wounds healed over
> Place of encounters and of the nightingale
> There are great open windows on the world
> that breathe spring and sing in unison

7

Body huddled in an old wool wrap
Face twisted to the taste of old plums
Lips curled up like sealed doors
She prays in silence through the cruel night
Her hands knotted
from wanting to give too much
Within these broken branches
a final ray of green sparks in the half light
Her paralysed legs tell the story
of a swallow who flew too fast
arrested in the exaltation of departure
her wings burned before attaining
the snow-covered crest
Mirror of a death she calls forth
as if seeking the anchor at journey's end
Her eyes alone still follow starlight,
the rhythm of flowers,
perfumed call of the song:
'She was born for the stars,
for the life breath flowing within her.
She was born to receive
the fruits of time.
She gave of herself, she suffered,
She traced a path, she opened doors
She walked in a closed city
Doors fell open
She spoke, she cried out
The walls gathered in
her solitary life.'

Sitting in the half light, immobile in her wheelchair, Nayla's mother listens to Hayate as she sings to the tune of her guitar. A sad, poignant melody. In the night, it moves over her face, her mother's painfully impassive mask, as it takes in the offering.

'I'd like to thank you for her,' says Nayla. 'You don't know how happy she must be. It doesn't show, but I know her. She's delighted. Your songs are so beautiful. Come, let's go into my room. I'd like to talk to you about the reading I've been doing.'

Hayate is always amazed at the magical power of music. It is a light that brightens the darkest corner, brings hope and reassurance. It is a utopia in action, which creates harmony, coherence and union. For Hayate, it is a personal means of reconciliation, the bridge linking differences. Music brings her peace.

She will have to sing today. Nayla has a sombre look, hesitates, then asks aggressively:

'The story you gave me to read, was that really your sister?'

'In a way, yes, as much as a fictional work can be autobiographical. It is one of my first works. It was painful to watch my sister suffering. I identified with her grief. I was reliving my wounds through hers. It's her and it's me. It's neither one nor the other, hence the title *In Between*.'

'Did she read it?'

'Yes, of course! My sister and I are very close, even if we don't always think the same way.'

'She accepted it? She allowed you to write about her, her marriage, her private life in that way?'

'She may not have accepted all of it, but she encouraged me to be honest with myself. That's why we're still friends and understand each other. My first novel is also partly autobiographical. Everything I write stems somewhat from my own experience. In order to express deep feelings, one must have lived the experience, don't you think?'

'I don't know, I'm not sure, Hay. I only know that I wouldn't allow someone to describe me as you've done. Now I regret having written the pages I showed you. You've got to tear them up.'

'I don't understand, Nayla. You really want me to destroy such

48

beautiful words that were so important for you to write ... the piece you just gave me? I'm convinced you have a real need to tell what you've written: it's a strong, authentic text. Why censure yourself like this?'

'I don't want to hurt my parents, my family – my father in particular. That's not the way to move forward.'

'But he has hurt you a lot! I, too, expressed painful moments with my father in my first novel. I didn't know if he would accept it. My sister had prepared him. He read my novel and apologised for having been so strict with a daughter as sensitive as I was. Since then, we've become the best of friends. If he had not understood, we'd have broken off contact. Isn't it worth it to be utterly honest towards others and oneself? How can we resolve political problems if we don't start with ourselves? Isn't one's private life also political?'

'I don't agree, Hay. It's not my approach. Besides, I also wanted to tell you that I don't like the novel you are writing about Lebanon. You would do better to write a historical novel based on factual incidents, go to the library of the Arab League, do some research on the causes and effects of war and build your novel around what is current. You will have more of an effect than with shocking sexual stories which don't add anything, or with repetitive images and stereotypical symbols.'

Nayla looks stubborn and closed. Hayate senses that it would be useless to continue; she would risk poisoning the conversation instead of resolving the differences between them. Perplexed, she watches Nayla who is nervously tapping a pencil on the pages of her novel.

'Did you read the whole manuscript?' Hayate ventures timidly.

'I told you that it bored me,' Nayla retorts. 'I didn't appreciate the few pages that I read. Here, take it back!'

And she throws the folder in the direction of her head. Hayate had wanted to say that you cannot judge a text you haven't fully read, but she feels such violence, such aggression coming from Nayla, that she can't speak. She picks up her novel and her guitar and leaves. Nayla has just enough time to add:

'And don't forget to return the pages I gave you, torn up.'

Hayate hurries down the stairs, heavy-hearted, with her eyes full of tears. What could have happened to change Nayla so dramatically? Maybe she didn't know her as well as she thought. Aïda and Rima had told her that Nayla had been transformed by her relationship with Hayate, which must have done her a lot of good because she was expressing herself as never before; that it was helping her to blossom.

She stumbles on the path that runs along the sea. Night has fallen and a cool breeze is blowing off the water. Hayate shivers. Aggression and violence, even expressed through words, cause her to turn inward. While others seem to enjoy what they call 'debate' – the argument deemed necessary to understand a problem – she runs from such discord which she thinks is futile. This has nothing to do with advice, proposals and suggestions given in good faith to help the other person to understand better and develop harmoniously.

Suddenly she is seized with fear, faced with her solitude, the empty house that waits for her in the night, the black sea in the darkness, and the wind which mounts towards a storm. She is anxious to return, to close the door and call Aïda. She is lucky to have such a friend! They understand each other; Aïda shares her desire for conversation without conflict and also shares her own feeling of solitude. Even with her daughter and companion, she is very alone. When you do not mentally share essential things with a special person, even though surrounded by people, you are always alone, murmurs Hayate.

She has arrived at the gate. She opens it, locks it behind her and crosses the garden. She opens the door to the house, turns on a lamp, locks the door, sets down her guitar and the manuscript, and immediately picks up the telephone. She tries in vain to make a call. There is no dialling tone. The telephone line appears to be dead. Of all the times for this to happen! Neither Aïda, nor Halima, nor other women who call from time to time, nor Lebanon, nor Paris, nor Chicago can reach her! She feels cut off from the world. If the line is not reconnected quickly, she will have to contact the landlord. This upsets her. She will try to see his wife.

She notices that she is trembling, that the discussion with Nayla has touched her much more than she had imagined. Why is she so sensitive? After all, maybe Nayla had thought she was doing the right thing! Perhaps she had truly thought it would help her to express her opinion in such a brutal way! Maybe it is just her way of saying things, even if Hayate finds them painful, even if it is alien to her positive, encouraging way of saying things without destroying, building so that creativity flows out, unhindered by obstacles.

She must take hold of herself, stop shaking, try to forget. She is not alone after all. She has her guitar, her songs. She has her writing. She has dear friends across the world who are thinking of her. No cause for panic. She feels a tight knot in her throat. She should drink something, try to calm down.

She prepares two fried eggs, opens a bottle of wine, and slices a tomato. Life is beautiful after all. After the meal, she will express her pain. She will hold her guitar and compose a sad song, with melodic chords, a chant from another land, a refrain woven with nostalgia, notes of love and birds, a vision of those far off friends that encircle her across time and space. She will try to give her suffering the ardour of Orpheus.

> Perhaps a song would suffice
> a morning on wings of stars
> a path woven with swallows
> two hands united in the evening
> for life to spring forth anew
> for the sky to redden with pardon
> for the earth to bring forth violets
> of springtime and reconciliation
> With my fingers the colour of wheat
> I have beaten the cadence of return
> farandole of peace
> I have kneaded the sand of the seas

51

that slips away indifferent to the ruptures,
the acts of violence and massacres
of my crazed country
There is within me a flame of love
which travels from East to West
Over cedar mountaintops
a great sad moon
has paused.

8

Black silhouette against a deep azure
Body folding, stretching, lengthening
tells its wounds, its scars
its joys and its sorrows
its tragedies and hopes
Body which dares to tell all
so truth may shine forth
so justice may triumph
so crushed flowers
might raise their heads
Life expressed in its flesh and its speech
like children running laughing across the beach
Beauty and strength in a face of oppression and
    desire
Muscles knotted in grief
smoothed by dreams
contemplation
Vision immortalised from within
Vulnerable existence, open
to winds, storms blowing across the plain
tides of a swelling people turned in on its fear
Arms, hands, legs describing
curves, lines, motifs that invent
confidence in tomorrow
and assurance the journey will be made
Words snatched from experience
dipped in the snow of a winter's suffering
You wander in the silence of words
Forever seeking the key to the journey

Images fashioned with allusions
Searching speech, giving itself
to the call of sensuality long ago stifled,
uncovered in these magical instants
You say that you needed much love, passion, faith
to regain the land crushed by war
to give the orange groves back to the city
Your words break shackles and anguish
reveal a dawn of spectacular light
New writing inscribing itself in time

A woman dressed in black stretches her arms, one skyward, the other out to the horizon. Now her form bends forward, her hands turn a slow circle, in harmony with her body's undulations. She curves, arches, draws herself in like a foetus. She remains there for the length of the refrain, words bright as a call:

I have waited long, long
on my road, the sun,
the bird flies off
a line parallel to my suffering
star shining in the night
I thought I saw a piece of sky
triangle of love trembling with joy
song of my divided desert
like these eyelids brushed with tenderness
that one kisses tenderly, slowly
trembling at their fragility
a fear of crushing them
It was only your shadow
Veiled vision, drapes of fabric undulating on the
    beach
Cries muffled by waves
violet rays on the horizon
small light among the clouds
For you have not yet been born
Oh my love, tender and marvellous

your life trembling under the dead leaves
perhaps I shall need to create you
imagine you taking form in absence
give to your arms the wings of a small bird
give to your voice the strength of gentleness
to your words confidence
and openness
give to your hands the light
of the fire hidden deep within me

The form unbends, starts to walk forward, forward, open palms,
full of light. Slender ankles, supple muscles, neck outstretched.
Her head drops down and rises proudly. Her locks of dark shining
hair quiver. Her deep brown eyes gaze into the room, while a red,
sensual mouth proclaims defiantly:

I lost my virginity like a bubble of air
a small constellation evaporated into the universe
Oof! I said, that day, bursting with laughter
seeing the contrite look
of this first lover
his evasive attitude
like a thief surprised during a night's visit
I am delivered
Never again will one come to claim his property
A harvest is on the plateau
grains ripening under a red sun
I am free finally free
to fill my hands and my mouth
with all of the colours of the river
Is that all that it is
a pinching in the stomach
a sadness quivering at the river's edge
an invitation to the journey
a door open to the breeze?
And I, seeking, still, as always,
this encounter that did not happen

The woman's body stretches out, her shoulders are splayed, her abdomen fills with air, chest forward, waist moving in rhythm; her stomach quivers; her legs shake, jump, slide. Now transfixed, now engulfed in trembling spasms, she vacillates, quivers, turns, sways and takes up her solemn walk, forward, ever forward. With a mysterious smile on her lips, she holds out hands and arms like a gift, like a bouquet thrown to the crowd, all the while saying in a mocking tone:

> We will no longer go to the woods
> My forest has been cut down
> The roses of my open garden have been gathered
> I wanted no doors or keys to guard it
> It is enough to love a melody on the buds
> to regain the poppy fields
> the place of truth
> and the brilliant star over grey dunes
> The one who wants me, believing he replants it,
> always off course, unseeing,
> will go from rose to rose
> from garden to garden
> following illusions
> as one follows a drug and then other poisons
> taken in by one's own lie
> But the man who will love me openly, naturally,
> will take my hand for an endless night
> We shall walk together on roads
> free with freedom

Hayate is entranced by Ahlame's performance evolving on stage. It is brilliant and powerful. She wonders if Ahlame is conscious of the power of the tenderness expressed, of repressed desires finally brought forth, of the universality of elements she uncovers, taboo subjects finally articulated, of love and hate mixed together, alternating anger and serenity, of the majesty of the words, and the harmony in her movements.

She is like a red bird of paradise in flight, a nightingale singing in the evening, a dove, its wings transparent as white clouds pierced with sky. She has the majesty and softness of roses, delicate thoughts, the surprise of cloves, the perfumed splendour of lilacs, the unparalleled quality of white lilies.

Deep in her thoughts, Hayate doesn't notice that the performance has ended. Aïda comes up and waves her hand in front of Hayate's eyes to bring her back.

'I told you, Ahlame is sublime. What she expresses is considered subversive in our society. Several insecure people who felt uncomfortable left during the performance. They couldn't stand to see or hear a person unmasking, expressing the forbidden.'

'I didn't notice the audience. I was too immersed in the show, captivated with Ahlame's presence. It's more extraordinary than I could imagine. Did she write the entire text? Was it really her . . . ?'

She is interrupted by Ahlame who faces her, laughing:

'Of course, it was me, *chérie*. Do you think that someone else could express what I've lived in my own skin, what I feel deep inside?'

'No, no, I'm convinced that only you could have conveyed those deep emotions, the richness of your experience, but I'm still amazed at the beauty of your performance. I just can't find words to describe it.'

'The admiration is mutual, *ma chère*! I've just finished your novel – it's quite amazing. I would like to write like that. I underlined so many sentences I would have liked to have written myself. They describe exactly what I feel. I tried so many times to reach you by phone. Where were you?'

'Me too,' exclaims Aïda, 'I tried to call you dozens of times. Is your phone out of order?'

'Yes, it hasn't worked for several days. I asked for it to be repaired. It's really difficult without a phone. It's hard to live alone. Without a telephone, it's unbearable. One feels cut off from the rest of the world, and especially from the voices of friends like you that I need so much at the moment. But what parts of my work are you referring to, Ahlame?'

'It's not an expression here and there. The novel is full of extraordinary passages. For example, when you describe your first physical contact with a man, and the description of the woman behind the veil and the one on the boat, and the young girls excised in the courtyard. It's also your very sensual way of expressing yourself, a violence within your softness. I am amazed by it!'

'And I'm still under the spell of what I've just seen. Your show is magnificent. Through mime and poetry you know how to express the importance of crucial moments in a woman's life, essential moments that have marked you. It is so important for women to put in words what has so long been repressed by society. History, families are afraid to see us claim rights which have been taken away from us. It's also the fear of our sexuality that you bring out with so much finesse.'

'Do you really think so? What a terrific compliment! If you only knew how much I have been criticised, and still am.'

'Wouldn't you like to carry on this discussion at my house?' interrupts Aïda, anxious about her daughter.

'I'd like to take Hayate to a place in the Médina where they are rehearsing a "hadra" scene for a film my mother is in. She'd love to meet you. Wouldn't you like to join us?'

'I have to pick up my daughter, who is waiting. But you go on and come to my house afterwards.'

'Come on,' cries Ahlame, who pulls Hayate along with her.

Night is falling on the rose and sand-coloured stones of the Médina. The narrow streets are still saturated with the heat of the day. A humid and dusty mist is rising from the alleys. Boys are playing soccer in the courtyards. Mothers call for them to return home for dinner. As always, the smells of olive oil, onions, eggs, fried fish and spicy harissa emanate from the houses. Ahlame takes her hand and leads her through the meandering streets of the Médina where it is easy to lose one's way. They walk on inspired by a bond between them that bridges time and space. They walk to give meaning to the darkness that invades the place. They walk, carrying hope, scars, dreams. There is within them so much strength and tenderness, so much subtlety and imagination.

They climb the streets which ascend and descend, open on to squares and pass cafés filled with men smoking narguileh, men with an insistent gaze, who scrutinise them so closely that the women lower their heads. They are measured aggressively, making them feel that this space is not theirs, that they should return home, or hide under a veil. Ahlame and Hayate pay little attention to them. They are looking for a place far removed from humiliation and meanness. They are heading towards a point of rupture and reconciliation that they know will lead them further still, into light.

They cross a market full of fabric, perfume and incense, full of people, a teeming crowd which grows heated, calls out. They are pushed from every direction, carried forward as if by waves. They find each other again in a narrow alley which opens on to a courtyard.

'It's there,' murmurs Ahlame, catching her breath.

She indicates a beautiful blue door, Tunisian blue allied with white, a dream of stars and sea, decorated with black studs and shiny mother-of-pearl. The door is open and vibrates to the rhythm of tom-toms under a languorous melody. Ahlame moves forward and draws Hayate inside. A group of spectators surrounds the actors and cameras focused on the women in this scene. The atmosphere is heavy with heat and sensuality. There is a smell of sweat, of perfume – violet, musk, jasmine, rose, benzoin – that rises from the bodies moving at the centre and from those who watch and join in, beat the rhythm, clap their hands and tap their feet.

Hayate and Ahlame are gripped by the magic of the spectacle, transported to another place, another time. Women with loose hair, bare feet, bare shoulders, dance in the centre. Frustration, disappointment, anger, bitterness and suffering are released from these bodies which tell their story openly and wait for deliverance. Behind them, an African orchestra plays themes built upon chanting rhythms. Flutes, violins, Tunisian horn and lute harmonise the plaintive melodies. Lyrics evoke sad love stories, the anguish of life, while tom-toms and derbakkés underline the violence of stifled passions, which erupt and lead finally to healing.

A woman in the middle of the circle is already in a trance. Her body bends and straightens with wild curves and contortions. Her hallucinating gaze is fixed upon the hypnotised crowd. Sweat pours from her forehead, neck and bare shoulders. Her long black hair is shining and damp and her dress stuck to her skin reveals a heavy, sensual body; from her mouth, plaintive sounds become cries of sorrow. She groans and twists. Her actions become quicker, accompanied by musical rhythms now unleashed. Her dance is a spell, an attempt to forget. She heightens the challenge by accelerating her tapping feet, her slides, dips and turns. She is short of breath, chokes on moaning sobs. She collapses on the floor like a wounded bird. She no longer moves, spent by her own trance, having lost the memory of all that had hurt her and kept her from healing. She has fainted, someone says; according to her, she recreates herself in the absence of consciousness. Some women from the group approach her, lift her up, wipe her forehead with cool water, fan her and carry her to the other side of the circle, outside the blinding light of the projectors. The cameras continue to film.

'Come,' says Ahlame, directing Hayate through the spectators. 'It's the end. Let's find my mother before she leaves.'

They have difficulty making a way through the crowd transfixed by the magic of the rite, bewitched by its spell. Other women in the circle continue the dance. They are the chorus of a Greek tragedy. They bring the passion to its height. The tom-toms accelerate the rhythm and reach their peak, then fall abruptly. A flute makes a plaintive call that serves as a coda, repeated many times, as the women slow their movements and then stop suddenly. The cameras stop filming.

Opposite them, in the circle, Hayate sees the face of a woman observing them and who seems to be waiting. That must be her. Ahlame joins her and bends to kiss her. Then she turns around and motions to Hayate:

'Mama, this is Hayate, the one I've told you so much about.'

Her mother looks at her, holds out her hand and smiles a bit reservedly. Hayate bends to tell her:

'What a pleasure to meet you. Ahlame talks about you so often. You have a marvellous daughter.'

The mother's eyes cloud over. She clasps her hand harder as if to convey feelings she dare not express. Hayate imagines what she must have suffered and still does. A generous, sensitive woman, she must have been caught between a demanding husband, her children's needs and the restrictions of daily life. Society permitted no escape.

'You are so beautiful, Mama,' exclaims Ahlame, putting her hand on her mother's hair. 'You put make-up on for the filming. Do you like your role?'

She becomes maternal with her mother, worries about her, is happy for this occasion which allows her to leave the house. She surrounds her with tender gestures. Hayate is touched by this scene, which reminds her of others equally moving.

> Woman with vibrant grey hair
> Woman with marked face telling a story
> Woman with slow gestures calming,
> comforting, renewing confidence,
> exasperating also, too much solicitude
> too much anguished attention
> Woman caught between a passionate girl
> in search of autonomy without limits
> discovering a new path
> thirsting for emancipation, seeking admiration,
> a husband, vehement, intransigent, the voice of
>   authority
> strict, severe in his criticism
> demanding, hard on himself and others,
> a society repressing desire,
> violent and brutal for those who contest it.
> She advances, anxious and serene,
> timid and courageous

Even so,
she believes she needs much patience
much love to live
She waits for the morning that will understand her

One night, Aïda takes Hayate to a real exorcism in the village of Korba. One of her friends goes there each week and suggests accompanying them; attending this rite which conjures demons is rarely possible without a personal introduction.

They leave Tunis around ten o'clock at night, arriving in Korba at eleven, and go to the sheikh's house. They leave their shoes outside the living room; they wait, sitting on pillows. One of the sons of the sheikh, a musician from the hadra orchestra, enters with a drum. He sits with them and explains the rhythms and words of certain sections. They contain religious verses taken from the Koran. This young man, aged about twenty, is open and sympathetic. His devilish eyebrows arch with each movement. His whole being emits a spell-binding magnetism. He answers all their questions without hesitation.

The sheikh appears, crossing the hallway. They must all go to the tomb of the marabout. They put on their shoes and take the car, accompanied by the sheikh's son. Most of the villagers go on foot. Aïda's friend knows the narrow, tortuous streets of the village well. Out of all the alleys come women with their heads covered, many in full veil, young people carrying drums and instruments, and men.

Aïda and Hayate cover their heads to enter the holy place. The women are separated from the men and led into the sanctuary, the holiest of holy places, the tomb of the marabout, the sheikh's ancestor. In this area – the place of the tomb – only women are admitted at this point in the ceremony. The men stay in the first room, the main room, situated near the entrance. Men and women are separated by a cloth – curtains hung on a wooden screen from one wall to the other, from floor to ceiling. These hide the space into which the women have been led. This women's place which Hayate enters is formed by two caves. Dark, round, humid and hot, it resembles a mother's breast, the vagina and the womb. One must lower one's head to slip more deeply into the second grotto, which is even darker, more humid and hot, where the ancestor's tomb is found.

Several women are already sitting there with a few 'sick ones' lying on the ground, prostrating at the foot of the white tomb. Slowly, Hayate grows accustomed to the darkness. The walls are whitewashed with candleholders hung on them. A man enters to place the candles and light them. Gradually the space lights up. A woman swings a vase containing burning incense. The white smoke gives off an acrid odour that is overwhelming. The air of the place becomes opaque, its atmosphere heavy.

Suddenly, Hayate is overwhelmed by a feeling of claustrophobia. She is suffocating and frightened to find herself restricted, as if kept there with no way out. This feeling of asphyxiation is intolerable. She seeks out Aïda and goes into the first cave, bumping into the bodies of women who are trembling in anticipation of the exorcism. Their sweaty hands express anguish, fear and the desire to communicate. She finds Aïda sitting, speaking to a woman accompanied by her daughter.

She sits down by them on the mat. She cannot understand every detail of this conversation in Tunisian Arabic, but grasps that the woman is talking about her life, unwanted pregnancies, her depression and illness. She looks about forty years old, laden with worries and overwhelming problems. Later, Aïda will tell Hayate that the woman is only twenty-six, already has four children, has just aborted the fifth, which depressed her and made her violent. When she realised that she was no longer in full control of her actions – that she had even threatened her children with a knife – she decided to come to the hadra to obtain exorcism of the demon. She had asked her oldest daughter to accompany her. Less than ten years old, the girl wears the serious look of an adult. Being female in this society is already weighing heavily on her fragile shoulders. She watches her mother with uncertainty.

On the men's side, the orchestra has started. The drums beat strong rhythms to accompany the recitation of religious verses to

63

incantatory, mystic, repetitive melodies. The effect is bewitching, hypnotising. Behind the cloth, the women render homage and encourage the chorus with strident youyous. The women's space is now full, the air becoming more and more impenetrable and suffocating, loaded with incense, smoke, candlelight, the cry of women, the beating of the men. The whole atmosphere vibrates with a crazed, hallucinatory music. Little by little, Hayate gets used to the feeling of asphyxiation created by the incense, the candles, the cries and the rhythm, which lead to a kind of hypnosis. She feels dragged into the frenetic circle and gets up, sways with the others.

A group of young women is there, surrounded by older women. With their hair loose and their eyes staring, they throw their heads up and down and back again to the rhythm of the drumbeats. The rhythm quickens and the head movements double their speed. They become frenetic, swept along by the youyous of the women who support them, call out and respond, intensifying the unfolding ritual and leading them to the exorcism. The pounding becomes stronger, the beating erupts; a kind of crazed hysteria is expressed through waves of spasmodic movements.

Suddenly Hayate is conscious of being dominated, carried along in spite of herself; she is no longer in control of her body and spirit. The feeling is uncomfortable; she refuses to continue. Approaching the cloth, she pulls back a piece of the curtain and watches what is happening on the other side. The son of the sheikh is sitting on the ground with his legs crossed. He beats a drum and recites and sings the words. His eyebrows dance over a demonic smile as he directs the exorcism to a hellish rhythm. The men's orchestra repeats the call to supernatural forces. The rest of the room is filled with men seated on the floor, their gaze fixed on the orchestra and the cloth separating them. Why don't they partake in the trance as well? Is dementia the exclusive right of women? What do they imagine takes place in that feminine space which they cannot see, that they have created in the image of the social division between the sexes that feeds their fantasies?

Hayate realises that she can see the men but they cannot see the women. Why this strategy? She feels manipulated, because the men orchestrate the hadra and pull the women into the trance. Not a single woman in the orchestra! The men are the actors in the exorcism. Are they not responsible for the dementia of the women they seek to exorcise? Has the oppression suffered by women not been engendered by the system of division and hierarchy? How is it that the women, being able to see what is happening on both sides, are not curious as she is, do not watch, do not rebel, but rather accept the role imposed on them? Do they have a choice? Why do these men not choose to see the feminine space, while the women can see the masculine one? The veil serves the same purpose. Is it the fear men have of woman – of her desire, her sexuality – that leads them to shut her in, to veil her? Or is it the perverse need to imagine without seeing the object of their fantasies that leads to this sequestering? Or can one analyse the hadra as a kind of mixed exorcism, carried out within permitted limits, and under the authority of an irreproachable person, the sheikh? Are men under the spell of the rite which has perhaps a therapeutic power for them as well?

Hayate turns back toward the women. Aïda is in the midst of the exorcism. She shakes her head and turns her entire body. She has placed herself among the possessed women and the older women who support them. She is holding hands with both groups. In contrast to the tense, nervous, anxious faces of the possessed and the maternal, domineering expressions of the older women, her face is serene. Later, Aïda will tell her that she did not sense the presence of the men and their space. The women had captured her full attention. A feeling of happiness and exaltation, stemming from the solidarity of the women, had submerged her. She had been plunged into the feminine atmosphere and into the dance and had forgotten her worries, her preoccupations. She had succeeded in chasing away all of her accumulated fatigue. Could the hadra be not just an exorcism, but also a therapy for the burdens of everyday life?

Hayate would like to attain this feeling of ecstasy like the others. She tries to move her head to the rhythm of these mystical pulses. She sits down like some of the women filled with hysteria and imitates their gestures. Next to her, the depressed woman sits with her young daughter. An enormous crease marks her forehead. She moans in her effort to let herself go. The girl does not know what to do and watches her mother with anguish. The tension in the body of this woman is intolerable. Hayate takes her hand to communicate her sympathy. Older women watch the scene. They approach the woman, loosen her hair and move her head in that delirious movement that leads to healing. The woman lets herself go and her body relaxes. The line on her forehead disappears; her mouth softens and her facial expressions take on a younger appearance. The women stand her up and help her to move her arms and legs to the rhythm of the accelerated beats and insistent youyous. She no longer appears to feel her body. The weight of her oppression has fallen away, her distress has left. She has been transported to a peaceful place. The accents of the rhythm and music intensify to a wild cadence which sweeps the women into an hallucination. Overwhelmed with ecstasy, she shakes and turns, bathed in sweat. Her hair is damp like that of the women who surround her and dance. The atmosphere is charged with the smell of sweat, wax and incense. Still curious, Hayate wonders if this woman lets herself go in the same way during intercourse. The mystical ecstasy – or *is* it mystical, because there is no contemplation of God? – rather the physical ecstasy, the separation of the body from suffering, a renaissance which replaces orgasm, calms the pain through a process which exacerbates it.

Aïda accompanies the woman in this process. Upon seeing her efforts, she approached her and took her by the hand to help. She supports and encourages her, aided by the other women, and warns her when she is in danger of falling or fainting. Hayate is touched by Aïda's feminist expression of humanism, by her goodness, her tenderness, her sensitive generosity. She would like to join her. She is held back by the feeling of rebellion that grabs her again; she feels dispossessed by a patriarchal power that controls the place and the sequence of events. Women have tried to escape from this through their solidarity, but still, their love feeds the fantasies of the men sitting behind the curtain.

Hayate returns to the separating cloth and what lies behind the veil. Has anything changed on the men's side? No, the room is still full of men hypnotised by the orchestra, plunged into their fantasy of what they imagine is happening behind the curtain. No man is in a trance as the women are. Do they have a different way of expressing their ecstasy? The musicians look electrified and drunk. The rhythms double their intensity and reach a crazy frenzy, an exhilarating height. They being the trance to an end.

The young girl has come up to the cloth and is watching the men through it. Hayate wonders what she is thinking. She is surprised by the girl's curiosity, while the other women seem completely disinterested with the men's side. The girl watched her mother for a long time, nervous, worried, afraid. She witnessed her going into a trance; she was fascinated by the spectacle of this being she did not know. Then she saw her being taken in hand by the other women and relax. She then regained her childhood and spontaneity. Is she being initiated into these secrets she will need, learning how to live through traumatic events that await her?

The youyous of the women, increasing in volume, become strident cries. The music builds and amplifies, reaching a deafening level. The thick smoke of incense comes in waves and fills the space, making one heavy and drunk. Some women lie on the ground, as if they have fainted. Hayate sees a man enter. At first, she does not realise that he is the sheikh. She is surprised by this intrusion, and even more surprised when she sees him go deep into the second cave where the tomb is and seize one of the 'sick ones' by the hair. He shakes her, whispers words in her ear and makes her speak. He spits in her face and rubs the saliva on it. Then he forces her to stretch out on the ground, puts one of his feet on her back, then on her arms and legs.

Hayate is petrified. She pinches herself to find out if she is dreaming or hallucinating. The scene is one of incredible violence. To Hayate, this moment appears to be the height of women's servitude. She is suffocating with anger and looks at Aïda to see if she has witnessed this and reacted to it! No, Aïda is completely taken with the dance; Hayate calls her, makes her watch. Aïda turns around to observe, but does not seem shocked. Does the act have another meaning? Hayate tries to understand. She is convinced that her reaction and feelings are justified even if the rite has other significance.

Now the sheikh returns to the cave where Hayate is. She sees him repeat the same gestures on each of the 'possessed' women. He approaches the depressed mother near Hayate and Aïda. He whispers verses from the Koran to her. He makes her speak. She pronounces inaudible words. He shakes her so that the words come out. She emits sounds. He seems satisfied and sputters, passing his hand over her face, throwing her to the ground. He repeats the walking on her body, an act which had Hayate beside herself with anguish. Hayate wonders about the effect of such treatment.

A young boy is pushed from the men's outside room to the women's space. He undergoes the same treatment as the 'sick ones'. Hayate learns later that he is one of the 'possessed', and when there are 'sick' men, they must enter the feminine space to undergo this operation of salvation. Could the feminine have power over madness and healing as over life and death?

On the way home, she hears another interpretation of the hadra. The sheikh shakes the possessed to make the demons leave. He speaks to the djinns to exorcise them and orders them to leave those they inhabit. He spits when the evil spirit has left to purify those who are ill and walks on the body to ensure that the devil has really left. Is this method of taking care of 'mad' people and neurotics perhaps more humane than shutting them up in asylums or placing them on an expensive psychiatrist's couch?

Aïda's friend describes the women's place as a feminist space! What he imagines behind the cloth – women taking their clothes off, completely hysterical and loose – he had even seen some climbing up the curtains and showing their breasts to the men – confirms Hayate's thoughts: because of the separation of the veil, the men's imagination can stoop to create all kinds of fantasies. It is impossible for a woman to climb the curtain; it reaches to the ceiling! But these remarks reinforce the extent to which the rite of the hadra can make people hysterical and hallucinate.

Hayate sees the depressed mother after the sheikh's intervention. Stretched out on the floor, she opens her eyes and shuts them hard and grimaces, shocked to find herself there. Her daughter approaches. Her mother asks where she is, does not remember anything. She shakes her head, rubs her eyes and brings her hands to her forehead as if suffering from a terrible headache. She tries to stand up and seems to hurt all over. Several women help her to stand. Hayate wonders what she will feel the next day when she gets up. Will she have found the answer to her troubles? Will she be calmer with her children, be at peace with her life? And for how long?

Hayate remembers an African American church in the United States. The Sunday service was similar to the hadra, without physical separation of the sexes, but the division was there all the same. The women enter into a trance during the ceremony when they are moved by the sermon or the Holy Spirit. They are taken with convulsions and cry out and tap their feet. If they faint, they are carried out of the room by the men. These are the women who have most supported the preacher with their encouraging cries: 'Praise the Lord! Hallelujah! Go ahead, brother!' during the service. Men also join in with their voices, but they are much more controlled.

Hayate had wondered if this was a way for women to resolve their problems without seeing a psychiatrist like so many Americans. To enter a trance and faint, would this allow them to express what had aggravated, frustrated and made them ill during the week? Do they then find themselves purified of their sins and troubles? Can they then turn the page and continue their life with more serenity? She also makes a connection between the hadra and the Catholic rite of confession. This also contains an outlet for suffering, not in the collective and yet segregated way of the hadra or certain African American churches, but individually. Does each society then have its own method for resolving its problems? Certain societies project on women the madness and demons that they must exorcise. Women take them in, confess them and in this way help society rid itself of them.

> Oh madness of despair
> A woman cradles her dead child
> She has shed a thousand tears
> A thousand stars in the night
> For his rebirth in peace one morning of love
> She walks along closed roads
> Separation, cloister, silence
> bridge of death
> torture
> Earth stopped by violence
> Sorrow as a gaze fixed upon the wall
> She dances until she forgets all
> chasing demons and disobedience,
> madness and rebellion all at once
> like the others
> she lets herself be trampled without understanding
> resigned to her suffering
> to the pain of others
> And I remain there, overwhelmed,
> outraged for these women
> sickened by the injustice
> not knowing how to give shape
> to all this pain
> wanting to find the bond of a plural unity
> the place of meeting and communication
> There are so many injuries
> so many scars on the words
> so many wounds in the dance
> rhythms of a silent, deaf earth
> Grieving for this pain,
> I gather life in.

9

In her small house in Salammbô, Hayate writes incessantly. How can she capture the faces of those she encounters? How can she recall all of their conversations? Make sense of the scenes she witnesses? How can she reveal, show to the reader the web which organises a story, the focal point which illustrates its meaning? How will she create a voice to rise above petty and destructive comments which can lead to cannon fire? How will she sustain this new voice among those who allow only hatred and violence?

Suddenly, she hears Nayla calling:

'Hayate, Hayate, are you there?'

She runs to open the door. Nayla appears shaken up. She trembles, saying:

'My mother has had to go to the hospital. She's very ill. Are you going to Tunis today?'

'I wasn't planning on it, but if you need something, I could go for you.'

'I have some meetings at the International Café I'll have to cancel; if you could go and tell them for me, you'd be doing me a big favour. I've got to take care of my mother. She may be let out of the clinic today. Someone's got to be with her around the clock.'

Nayla makes a list of names; Hayate recognises several from the group she's already met. Hayate offers her something cool to drink. Nayla is very nervous and chain-smokes. She sits on the edge of the wall that encloses the courtyard outside the kitchen door.

'I'll have to get a replacement for my classes and a leave of absence to take care of her.'

'What a burden for you.'

'No, not at all. It's a joy! She's given me so much. At least I can return the favour to some small degree. It's *Nissa*, the women's journal, that's bothering me; it's just beginning and the women need me.'

'When is the first issue?'

'We were hoping for next week, but I don't know if it's possible. We've had so many problems.'

'They told me . . . the lack of unity, the group is divided . . .'

'There are some remarkably well-written articles, but others are very poor. We should be able to choose which ones to include. As for me, I don't have a clear idea of what we need any more and I'm tired of working on it.'

'Everyone's nerves seem to be on edge lately. But the theme of equality in relationships is a fine one and we have to fight to bring it about despite difficulties, don't you agree? I'm also a little disappointed because I had an article I wanted to publish, but it just wasn't possible.'

'Well, I've got to tell you, Hay; a Lebanese man or woman living in the U.S. is always under suspicion.'

Hayate is surprised by this direct affront. She wonders if Nayla understands the impact of what she has just said, and why she is asking for a favour under the circumstances. Maybe she feels such strong friendship for Hayate that she wants to warn her. For a while now, Hayate has become increasingly aware of the growing tension between her and the other women, misunderstandings she attributed to the group's internal disputes. Suddenly she is afraid, anticipating danger.

'Why?' she asks. 'Is a Tunisian man or woman living in France considered suspicious?'

'It's not the same thing. Right now the U.S. is playing a game of dirty politics internationally. Its government nourishes and supports fascist regimes and police states. And it gives unconditional aid to Israel. It supports racist and expansionist Zionism one hundred per cent.'

'One would think that an intelligent person could distinguish between a people and its government and would be able to consider that a Lebanese man or woman living in the United States might be pursuing resistance activities. Because of such endeavours, American opinion changes and bad ideas are modified. Even if the effect is minimal, does one have the right to put it down?'

Nayla reddens, withdrawns and cloaks herself in a protective shell.

'I have to go. In fact, I just came to take back my books and also I'd like to tear up the manuscript I gave you.'

Hayate is saddened to see Nayla turning away. She hopes it is based on fatigue due to her mother's illness. Once hard times have passed, once Nayla has regained her smile of former days, she will try to break through again. Hayate leaves the room and returns with a package.

'Here! I had put everything in a bag that I hoped to bring you the next time I stopped by your place.'

Nayla takes the package and leaves the way she came. She retains her look of sombre days. Hayate's heart is heavy. What Nayla has told her has not been reassuring. She puts away her books and notebooks and puts some things in a bag. She will spend the night with Aïda. She needs to be in touch with someone who understands her, in whom she has complete confidence. She knows these feelings are shared and they can count on each other. Frustrated, as well, by a phone still out of order, despite promises of repair a few days earlier, she has forgotten how much patience is necessary for day-to-day living.

She locks the house, walks along the sea, a peaceful blue with green highlights, speculum of a life in turmoil. Only a few clouds stretch out across the sky. Ideal weather for a walk along the coast. In a few days, a few weeks, it will be too hot and everyone will want nothing more than to dive into the cooling waves. She never tires of this beautiful landscape which reminds her of Lebanon: bays with their well-defined coasts, fishing boats, sailing boats, small white houses with round arches terraced in the pines.

Breathing deeply, she recalls Aïda, her breasts naked to the wind, advancing through the waves. There are so few women, so few men and women who manage to remove the shackles of the past. Freedom is harder to accept than slavery. It is easier for a woman to be locked away in the house and to veil herself before going out than to have to fight for her daily bread. Hayate wishes Nayla would express her innermost thoughts, those which still hide under the surface. She is also conscious of the price to be paid for this freedom: solitude, marginalisation, humiliation, petty revenge from a society which does not allow its creative voices to express their rebelliousness and their anger. Incessant murmuring voices curbing the blossoming, the fullness of feelings. She has the impression that Nayla feels obliged to justify her actions by a sense of duty she mistakes for being humanitarian.

Hayate reaches the train station. She buys her ticket and boards the train. Pushing her face up against the windowpane to conceal her tears, she is afraid of the future, as much for herself as for her country. It seems so difficult to change minds, to modify relationships of power, to abolish the clan system, to dispel pettiness. Will she be able to live differently, and will her country be able to get out of the cycle of mounting violence leading to the Apocalypse?

The sea is a calm azure. It meets the lagoon sleeping under its grey-green covering, an ages old crossing. Seagulls pass over slack water. They dive and come up again, telling their stories to the light. Their turning is gracious as legend. Hayate would like to feel the subtlety of a swallow who leaves without regret in autumn. She would like to rid herself of suffering.

The train enters the station in Tunis. Hayate gets off and takes long strides down Bourguiba Avenue. Men stare at her openly; she hardly notices them, as she is plunged in sad reflection. The rows of flowers which usually fill her with joy are without colour today, without scent. She enters the International Café. She finds Nayla's group and delivers the message. There is no warmth in their reception. Hayate hesitates but seeing no other table free, she sits down and orders coffee. The faces are sombre, the discussions relentless.

'What courage she had, that young Lebanese woman, Sana, in that suicide operation which killed several Israeli soldiers in southern Lebanon.'

'Yes, but the Israeli reprisals were quick. They opened fire on several southern villages, killing innocent civilians.'

'It's the fault of the United States which supports that fascist and racist regime; they send weapons to ensure their strength and power.'

'Yes, and what about all the funding, the money they give to the Hebrew State – the fifty-first state of America?'

The criticism is implicitly directed at her. In the past, Hayate would not have taken it that way; she tends to take a naive stance with people known to be political activists. But after Nayla's warning and the cold reception, she cannot help but feel targeted. She would like to ask which country in the world did not send arms to the region, particularly to Lebanon, in order to feed a conflict for which everyone sheds crocodile tears but to whose agony they are indifferent. However, as always in these situations of verbal violence, she remains silent, incapable of taking part or breaking up the virulence of the argument.

'What's happening to Lebanon could happen to Tunisia,' someone adds. 'Geographically, we're also at a crossroads. We're under the influence of the U.S. We support their interests in the Mediterranean and through that we defend the State of Israel. We have just taken in Palestinians exiled from everywhere, and especially from Lebanon. Put all these elements together and it looks as though we're on the road to inevitable conflict.'

All of a sudden, Hayate feels a hand on her shoulder. She turns around and Rima is there with her brilliant open smile. Her eyes sparkle behind her glasses. What a happy turn of events! As with Aïda, Hayate has complete confidence in her. Her direct and profound way of speaking, her gift of integrating different ideas, her sense of equity, her way of taking things in hand without ever denigrating or intimidating the other person, her acceptance of contradictory ideas – all of this has resulted in her being given increased responsibility among various groups of men and of women. She was elected President of the Union of Arab Journalists for the entire Arab world. It is rare for a woman to be elected leader of a group with a majority of men in it, and not only in

Arab countries. But there is more – the powerful position she has achieved, which would have corrupted another person, has not changed her simplicity and genuine nature. She does not take herself more seriously just because she is successful, and she knows how to laugh even at the most difficult moments. She can ease a strained atmosphere while remaining concerned and attentive to current problems. She could not have appeared at a better time.

'I was looking for you,' Rima says to her. 'I tried calling you several times.'

'My phone's been out for a week. It was supposed to be fixed. If Nayla hadn't had this emergency, I wouldn't have come. I'm so happy to see you.'

'Me too! Listen, I've got some questions to ask you. I'm preparing an article on that young Lebanese woman in the suicide operation, and I'd like to compare her actions to the other Lebanese woman, just as brave – the one you spoke to me about – the one who, in the midst of bombings, organised a peace march for Lebanon while you were there.'

'What a great idea!'

'I think so! The stories of these two women fascinate me. They have both proved incredible heroism in an attempt to save their country, one by violence, the other through active non-violence. And they both failed. You said the peace march was stopped short, right? I need more information.'

'In concrete and practical terms, they have perhaps failed, but not symbolically. Their acts will always be remembered. As for me, I opt for non-violence, the peace march, because I don't see any other solution for Lebanon.'

One of the members of the group who has overheard, explodes:

'How can you say that when the aggressor is Israel? To its violence, we have to respond with violence.'

'Israel is not the only country to attack Lebanon,' Hayate bursts out. 'And even if that were the case, personally I would not respond with violence. Revenge entails more vengeance. Blood calls for more blood; today's victims become tomorrow's executioners. Israel is a good example. I would have liked to organise a peace march for Lebanon here too, but no one seems to understand what's at stake.'

'I'm very interested,' Rima breaks in, 'and I'd like you to give me details concerning what you did there to organise the march. Let's go to another table to talk about it.'

A little table near the bay window has just become empty. Rima rushes over to claim it. Hayate follows her and orders another coffee and a cup of tea for Rima. Paper and pen in hand, she continues:

'I want as many details as possible to show the parallels between the actions of these two women. One chose to affirm life through peace, the other gave her life believing she was saving others from death. I would have liked to tell Sana to join the peace march.'

'I did meet Imane, the young Shiite woman who inspired the peace march, when I was in Beirut last year. We were both at the Research Institute for Women in the Arab World. I knew her to be a very calm, poised woman. When she took this initiative, we were all surprised by her confidence, her enthusiasm and keen interest. This young woman, soft-spoken and reserved, who enjoyed taking care of children, had suddenly acquired a surprising amount of self-assurance. In a few days, she managed to organise the entire demonstration – posters, banners. She mobilised a crowd of people from all over the place and from all classes, clans and faiths. In the beginning, it was mainly women who responded to the call. Imane was co-ordinating her efforts with those of Laure, a woman from East Beirut, from the other side of the demarcation line. She was a lawyer known for her long campaign of non-violence to counter the war. The march had as its only slogan: "No to the tenth year of war. No to war. Yes to life."

I lived through days of euphoria and happiness that are difficult to describe. The hope that filled us was like a calm, starry night in the midst of our torment. We had the impression we were finally sailing towards the port of reconciliation and forgiveness. Each person to whom we spoke about the project already seemed aware of it and took it up with enthusiasm, deciding to participate and suggesting others join us. In the beginning, the men were sceptical or scornful, but then they leaned in our favour. In time, many joined us. We were all to meet at the line of demarcation, at the Museum passage, early in the morning. Children dressed in white would hold up a banner touting the chosen slogan, and we would release doves. Thousands of people on all sides were to participate. I remember the Druze woman who used to clean my flat once a week. The year before, she had seen her family massacred by Christians in the mountains. She was so enthusiastic about the march that she had brought about twenty people she knew. I could give you lots of other examples, if you like.'

'So why didn't this march take place?'

'The leaders of the clans, the militias, weren't too happy about it, of course. I remember the declarations made by the head of the Druze militia. He claimed we weren't sincere! To him, as to others, sincerity was measured only by violence. And so terrible bombings on the city took place the night before the day chosen for the march, causing dozens of deaths and hundreds of casualties. In the morning, the city smelled of powder and blood. The guns could still be heard rumbling in the distance. Ambulance sirens tore through the silence of a city reduced, once more, to despair in a repetition of violence. It was enough to drive you crazy. We took the risk of leaving the shelters to confirm that once again the sky had taken on its black veil of sadness.'

'What was Imane's reaction?'

'Of course she was very discouraged, but she told me that the march was alive in the hearts of all Lebanese who rejected war, and that one day peace would triumph. As for her, she would carry on with her undertaking. It's what she's still doing. When I saw her this year, during a stay in Lebanon, she explained to me how that march had generated a long list of signatures of thousands of Lebanese who said "no" to war. The banner had been set on the line of demarcation. People can be killed, but not words nor faith.'

'I'm thinking about Sana's act. She chose to throw herself at the

Israeli tanks. What was she feeling when she decided to do it? Was it sadness for Lebanon, for her country occupied by foreign powers? How is it then that she belonged to the Syrian Popular Party and that it is Syria, another occupier, which praises her martyrdom and gave her name to a street in Damascus? Did she legitimise pro-Syrian feeling through her link to the Arab nation? Was it anger? Was it bitterness? Can one be bitter at that age? She was only seventeen. Was it a desire for heroism? You know the passions of youth – she stated on a video recorded before she left that she felt a rejoicing similar to that of her wedding day celebration.'

'As Sana said, violent death often evokes the wedding celebration. There is a sexual dimension to the horrors of war. The thought of it makes me shudder. I find it repugnant. In the video, she tells her parents not to cry, but rather to rejoice as if she were going to celebrate her marriage. In death and marriage, there is a bursting, a blossoming, both towards death and towards life. Maybe that's what she meant to say, to explain her comparison. I can't imagine what animated Sana, especially since I didn't know her. But I can say that the feelings which supported Imane were sweetness, goodness, generosity, love and care for others, as well as respect for difference, tolerance and the desire for reconciliation. She had a particular talent for reaching out to children; they adored her. She managed to lead them without ever raising her voice.'

'If you hadn't told me about Imane, I'd still be unaware of her existence, while the media keeps repeating the story and pictures of Sana.'

'It's always the same. Violence and death make the front page, while courageous and visionary acts capable of transforming the world and its corrupt values go unnoticed, untold. The press loves death; it uses and reinforces public taste for the macabre.'

'The media is dominated and controlled by men. They'd rather conceal acts such as Imane's, which threaten their authority and their idea of the world. Those acts question their very existence and their justification of violence and war, while a woman like

Sana reassures them by taking up the same argument, the same ideology. This is why one of the heads of the Syrian Popular Party was able to state, speaking about her: "Women also have a political role to play."'

'It's appalling. The wars of "liberation" have used and continue to use women. They send them back to the kitchen afterwards. Women are used. It's time they recognised this and opposed the role. It's time they consciously chose a part they can and really want to play.'

'It's also time for women journalists – women with jobs in the media – to adopt other points of view and to stop repeating what men want them to say.'

'Is there censorship to prevent them from speaking out?'

'There's an internal censorship, a self-imposed way of thinking we use when we want to please and be accepted by society and the men who judge us.'

'I understand the importance of the journal you've just created. There, you are among your own and can really express what bothers you freely, without fear or the desire to please.'

'You idealise our journal a bit. What you're saying is partially true, but male discourse, the power games, also exist among women who adopt masculine ways of analysis. It's easier to copy than to invent, easier to repeat a conventional analysis than to look for new interpretations. Women are afraid to assert themselves, to formulate new opinions. They're blocked, paralysed by a system in which consensus is established. When they succeed in breaking the shackles that hold them down, when slowly they finally express themselves, they'll discover that what they have expressed, or tried to express, is scorned, marginalised by journalistic power which will ignore our paper, for example, saying you should buy the one "which has proved itself" instead. Attitudes can't change overnight. As for me, I think that while I'm waiting, I've got to work for both the recognised papers and the marginal ones.'

'Will the article you're writing on Sana and Imane be accepted by an established paper?'

'Probably not. I'll have to give it to ours.'

'These problems seem insoluble. How can we reach people, readers, the public, with different ideas, information, analyses that could open their eyes, if they can't read what we write?'

'Working class people who read are in any case in the minority. Things progress slowly – it has to start among women. Our mutual support is a strength which will allow us to have an impact on male-dominated areas. We will change things gradually, have an influence on public opinion. We can't hope for more. It's not all that bad.'

Rima smiles, her face brightens. There is strength and intelligence in her eyes, determination and calm. Hayate thinks about the success of her work as a journalist in so many areas, of her personal life where she is able to combine independence and complementarity, passion and friendship, linking her emotional life to her professional life in a relationship that is lasting and allows her to blossom.

> Flower of our beaten earth
> You speak the magic of pardon
> the sensitivity of the talisman occulted
> through the shadow invading our planet
> the delicate renewal carved of intelligence
> the desire to understand, to communicate
> to find words to appease quarrels
> On the road blocked by the tempest storm
> you open a bridge of peace
> In the villages and camps burned by napalm
> you trace symbols of reconciliation
> Beyond the shackles and the chains
> you draw a city rising from the ashes
> In the furrow of non-violence
> you sow recognition of the other
> Tolerance
> accepting difference
> you flow a river of peace across the earth

rebounding in sweetness regained
rose water healing the wounds
Even when you are weak with others' anger
you enlace your words with a taste of violet

10

When Hayate leaves the International Café, night has already fallen and it is raining. She looks for a taxi, difficult to find in this weather. People are hurrying in all directions. The buses are full. Women call out, speak sharply to their children, hugging their belongings and gesturing to taxis that do not stop. Hayate attempts to do the same without success. Even if the buses were accessible, she would not know which one to take. She is supposed to go across town. Running in the rain at this hour seems impossible. She waits, hoping that a taxi will stop . . . she waits. She has forgotten the patience you need for public transportation. She watches the street covered in puddles of water, the annoyed passers-by who call to each other, cry out, swear, spit on the ground. From time to time, a gust of wind turns her umbrella inside out and the rain drenches her. Cars splash her when she jumps to the curb to wave to likely taxis. Her feet are soaked. Her hair and dress are wet. The blowing wind is freezing. She should have dressed more warmly. But who could have imagined this morning that the storm would be such a violent one? The sky and the sea were so peaceful. She shivers and wonders if she shouldn't try to call Aïda from a nearby hotel.

All of a sudden, a miracle! A taxi stops. She runs to the door, climbs in. A gust of wind closes the door on her umbrella, part of her dress is stuck in the door. The driver grumbles about the storm, the future, life in general. Hayate tells him her destination and asks him why there are so few taxis in this weather. He answers that there are lots of taxis, but they are all taken or have been reserved by telephone. Hayate explains the very practical Lebanese system. You can stop any taxi, even if there are already passengers inside and take it if it is going in the direction you want. And it is cheaper! A conversation follows that Hayate would

83

have many occasions to repeat with taxi drivers during her stay in Tunisia.

'Ah, Lebanon! You come from Lebanon? What's happening there is horrible.'

'Are you keeping up with the news? What's your opinion?'

'It's the Palestinians' fault. Here we're really afraid they'll destroy our country like they have Lebanon.'

'It's not only the fault of the Palestinians. Besides, Palestinians didn't choose to go to Lebanon, just as they didn't choose to go to Tunisia. The set of circumstances that took their country from them, that took away their identity and passports, has made them aggressive. It's made them push even harder for their legitimate claims that no one wants to hear. They're not the most guilty. In Lebanon, several factions are fighting and civilians are the victims.'

'They say that over there Christians are killing Muslims. The Christians are not Arab. They should return to Europe or go to America.'

'There are Arab Christians. I'm an Arab Christian.'

The driver is surprised.

'What? How is that possible? An Arab is Muslim.'

'Don't you know that the three religions of the Book – Judaism, Christianity and Islam – come from this part of the world? The Copts in Egypt – they are Christians, too.'

'The Copts are not Arab. Arab Christians? It's unthinkable!'

'I've just told you that I am one of them. Muslims, Christians and Jews worship the same God, but in different ways.'

'Jews took land from the Palestinians and the Palestinians are causing trouble here.'

'You only mention Palestinians. Aren't you afraid of other groups in Tunisia?'

'Other groups? Which ones?'

'The Islamic Fundamentalists, for instance.'

'Yes, yes, we're afraid of them, too. They want to impose their way of praying, dressing, living; they want women to wear the veil again. But the Koran doesn't say that women have to be veiled.

84

The veil was for the wives of the Prophet, peace be upon him! That is why Bourguiba outlawed it. He was right.'

'You know the Koran well. How is it that you don't know that the Bible and the Koran are very close and that both come from this part of the world?'

The driver is perplexed. Engrossed in the conversation, Hayate had not realised they were already in the Bardo. She points out the road to Aïda's house. They arrive. She pays, thanks him and gets out of the taxi. The storm has calmed somewhat, but the road is muddy and covered with water. She knocks. Aïda appears, smiling.

'You're soaked, my poor dear,' she cries out upon seeing her. 'Come in, change your clothes and warm up.'

'It took so long to find a taxi and I couldn't phone you. I hope you didn't wait for me to eat. My shoes are so dirty; I'll leave them at the door. Do you have something for me to put on?'

Aïda quickly finds her some things to wear. Her daughter and Ahlame are there. Hayate is happy to see them.

'I didn't know that you were here, Ahlame! What a nice surprise!'

'I'm the one who's pleasantly surprised. I really wanted to talk to you. Since our last meeting, I've made so many plans. I'd love to tell you about them. But rest first. Come and warm up.'

Aïda brings socks, a big sweater and a towel. She helps Hayate to dry off.

'Of course we waited to eat. Fortunately! I knew you'd make it. I made couscous.'

'Your couscous is always delicious,' declares Ahlame cheerfully. 'Let me serve it.'

Hayate feels surrounded, warmed, comforted by the loyal friendship of these women which makes her forget the difficulties of recent weeks. She talks about her day and her discussions with Hayla, Rima and others at the International Café. She pours out her heart. Ahlame and Aïda listen during dinner.

Suddenly, Ahlame interrupts:

'You know, I came for a specific reason that I'll tell you when we've finished eating. I'm glad you're beginning to understand what is happening. For some time I've wanted to warn you about the risks you run that you don't seem to be aware of. There are some unfortunate things happening you should know about. But finish your meal in peace. We'll make herb tea and talk about it. I've had some serious problems in my life lately, too. I'm at the end of my tether.'

'We're all fed up,' adds Aïda. 'If only you knew the problems this journal is giving me!'

'I know, I know,' says Ahlame, 'because I've left the project, resigned. I couldn't stand any more quarrelling. You have to be a masochist to take it.'

'It's not that,' says Aïda, 'but we have to persevere and let time take its course. Relationships don't change from one day to the next just because we've decided they will. We must have patience and work at it.'

'Work, I can do plenty of, but patience for imbeciles, no thank you! I'll go and make the tea.'

Ahlame disappears into the kitchen. Aïda clears the table:

'Stay here with my daughter. Rest, and dry off near the heat while we put things away.'

Hayate lies back on some large pillows. She tells a story to Saïda, Aïda's daughter, who listens, wide-eyed.

'Once upon a time in a country with fabulous cedar forests, with fields of wild flowers which scented and coloured the mountains with a thousand perfumes and reflections, there was a young girl with dark eyes and curly chestnut hair. She lived in a peaceful home on the edge of a cliff overlooking the sea. She was surrounded by a loving family. She attended school during the week and at the weekend she would run in the forest and flowering fields. She spoke to the birds of the forest who flew over the fields in search of food. She loved one bird in particular. He was beautiful with rich violet and green plumage and they said he came from a distant island, from beyond the seas. Many years ago an immigrant had brought a couple of them in a cage he had

86

opened upon his arrival. The forest was filled with these beautiful green-violet amazon parrots that told stories.

'One day, the little girl was walking in the forest and she saw her amazon lying on the ground, its wings covered with blood. She came closer and saw that the bird was still trembling. It had just received a lead bullet in the heart. She caressed the bird, trying to revive it. She spoke to it, hoping that a sound would spring from the open beak. But the bird had died. The little girl took it home, holding it carefully in her hands. Her house was filled with turmoil. Her father declared that from this time forward, she was not to venture into the forest alone. Her mother seemed relieved to see her back at home. Her brothers explained that some men from a neighbouring hill had declared war and that they had decided to construct trenches to protect the house and even to go off and fight if necessary.

'The little girl understood that her life had changed forever. The bird's death signified the end of her carefree existence. She put the bird in a box she decorated with flowers and butterflies of rainbow colours. As she ran to the garden to dig a hole under the apple tree, she saw her brothers working, digging on the other side of the fence. Already, the sounds of machine guns and cannons could be heard on neighbouring mountains. She spoke to her bird, showering it with tears. She whispered to him to return to his faraway island and to tell all the birds to form a chain of peace to stop the war.

'The night was eventful. Everywhere battles had raged destroying houses and burning forests. The little girl and her parents had taken shelter underneath their house. In the morning, her mother had taken advantage of a lull in the fighting to bring them food. The respite was short-lived. During this brief period, some of their neighbours had asked for shelter since her family's house was better protected and had a more comfortable basement. They spoke of the destruction they had witnessed. No one would have imagined that such a tragedy could occur in such a peaceful country. They described the charred trees, entire fields that had been devastated and a thick cloud of birds fleeing across the sea. The little girl listened, listened and trembled, hoping that all of her friends had been able to escape to more clement skies.

'For three days and three nights, they had to hide, to remain in the basement, shaken by explosions, frightened by all sorts of horrifying noises never before heard. The house and the mountain shook as if moved by an earthquake. The few supplies they had been able to take underground had run out; her mother proposed risking a trip to the kitchen to bring something below. Her father worried about his sons and wanted to explore the area surrounding the house.

'On the morning of the fourth day, a cease-fire was announced on the radio. When calm had apparently returned, family and neighbours peeked outside. The little girl ran out to the garden. She stopped in surprise in front of the tree under which she had buried her bird. The apple tree was covered with white and rose-coloured flowers. A sweet perfume arose from the delicate corollas of its branches. This tree bloomed in the midst of a sinister landscape – entire fields destroyed and burned, charred trees, the forest reduced to cinders, fallen houses, broken windows, fires still burning upon the mountain. The apple tree was standing there bursting with life, beauty, rebirth and hope. The little girl approached the place where she had buried the violet-green amazon. She bent toward the tomb, murmuring: '"Thank you, thank you."'

'Thank you for the beautiful story,' cried Ahlame, entering with the tea tray. She sits on a pillow and begins to pour the green-gold tea.

'At last! I've been so anxious to tell you what has been weighing me down. What's happening to you happened to me last year; what you are saying and doing is disturbing – so they talk behind your back and accuse you of all kinds of things in order to sling mud at you and make your words and actions suspect. I've had enough of this country. I've accepted a grant to study in France. I'm leaving in a few weeks.'

'What are they accusing us of?'

'They said that I was a loose woman, a lesbian and a husband stealer. They're saying you've organised orgies, stolen your friends' lovers and have sold yourself to the CIA.'

'It's astonishing; except for the CIA, all of this slander concerns sex. Have you figured that out?'

'Yes, of course. One slanders someone else because of what one fears inside oneself. Sexuality is expressed so badly in our country that people become jealous of those who are open and free. They attribute to another person all sorts of personal desires, goals that they would like to achieve, but that they don't dare admit. In a presentation I made last year, I spoke openly about virginity, about my rejection of motherhood, about the jealousy of women among themselves, which goes back to the relationship they have had, and continue to have, with their mother. I had tried to analyse in depth the psychological aspects which lead to the stifling of sexuality in our society. In your writings and your presentation on Lebanon, you have also emphasised the relationship between men and women and sexuality. Our approach makes them uneasy because it goes directly to the heart of the problems – to what is essential, to the intimate, to personal relationships. People can't take it if you put your finger on what hurts in their private life, asking people to change in this area. It's much easier to speak to people and to mobilise them on a political level than on a personal one. To put the blame on external forces is much more convenient than to take a look at yourself, to be self-critical and try to change.'

Hayate is shocked by what Ahlame has just said. She has felt uneasy for some time. She had realised that certain women were not as friendly and open as they had been at first, but she put this down to tiredness and everyone's anxiety. She was far from suspecting the cruel things being said behind her back.

'I must understand what is going on,' she says. 'For a start, can you explain to me why my short story *In Between* is so disturbing? Nayla told me that I never should have written like that, talking about my sister, her husband and my family as I did – that I had no right to do so. She finds it indecent.'

'Your story is very good. It's impeccable in its formal style,

89

concise, and at the same time very poetic. For me it is your best work. It's a touching story, so true-to-life, and so well written. In just a few pages, you tell the truth about the oppression of women in our societies and you have dared to do so in a personal way, basing it on real, lived experience. It's deeply touching because it goes straight to the problems, without beating about the bush. If you had masked your message in nebulous sentences, veiled words, ambiguous identities, some people would have applauded you. Not me – I prefer a thousand times over what is direct and I like the simplicity of your style. Truthfully, I like your story better than your novel where you mix poetry and prose. And what does indecency mean anyway? It's rebellion – wanting to change things by breaking with old established customs. It makes people afraid, because it questions everything. But it is the only way to move things forward, to transform human relationships, between women and men, among women and among men. I think that one must dare to be indecent. And what does it mean not to have the right to say certain things, precisely those things one must have the courage to say? Why censor? Is there not enough censorship in our society, without adding our own?'

'Yes, there is a big problem in that area. There is self-censorship for a lot of women. They are afraid to speak and write because they would be obliged to criticise, denounce, accuse those near to them. It's a difficult step to take. One must have a lot of courage to question those one loves and with whom one shares close relationships. That is why so many women across the world have so much trouble liberating themselves. Contrary to the history of blacks or the labour force, they entertain amorous relationships with their oppressors. I think too that if we are afraid to hurt those we love, it's that we do not love enough and we do not trust them. True love must communicate these vital things, don't you think?'

'Unfortunately, it doesn't work like that. We fear others because we fear ourselves and are afraid to understand ourselves, to love ourselves, to assume our freedom. You have chosen to live free. You left your country when its customs stifled you. You didn't hesitate to break ties with your roots and create a life for yourself alone elsewhere and without anyone else's help. You had immense courage that others don't have. I admire you and want to do the same thing. But you frighten those women who do not have the same courage. So they prefer to drag you through the mud.'

'I would understand the slander coming from people outside the feminist movement. But, if I understand correctly, it's coming from women who are conscious of the problems of women, who should have adopted the slogan: "the personal is political".'

Aïda, who has just come in, pours a cup of vervain and joins the conversation:

'Almost all of us come from political movements of the left. Our speech is determined by Marxist ideology. We have managed to eliminate male dominance by creating our own movement, but we haven't yet found language that doesn't reflect patriarchal domination.'

'We'll never find it!' declares Ahlame. 'We are much too occupied with criticising each other, cutting each other down, slandering each other. I can't bear these accusations and misunderstandings any longer. The atmosphere is eating away at me and keeps me from developing further, from creating, blossoming. It is clipping my wings, my spontaneity. Instead of being encouraged for my ideas, I only come across destructive criticism, disapproval, slander, defamation. I have decided to leave, to be free, finally free.'

'If you think that it will be better elsewhere,' cries Aïda, 'you're fooling yourself. We have to try to change things here; if we don't, nothing will change.'

'I've just told you that I'm exhausted because I can't see a single positive result. I prefer to try my luck overseas, to discover the land of opportunity, where doors are open and ears attentive to those with ideas and imagination.'

Hayate says nothing. She feels sad and discouraged. It seems so difficult to go forward, to try to live differently, to help others to break their chains without causing pain. To put the finger on the wounds in order to take away the hurt and not deepen it. She is conscious that the road she has chosen is long and full of thorns.

She looks at these two women who have opened their hearts and door to her. Women like them are hope for Tunisia, for the Arab world, for the world in general. They are both right: Ahlame wanting to live her life elsewhere, where she will perhaps find understanding and approval, and Aïda wanting to stay and fight, to work toward the realisation of her dreams for a better society, even if that means facing tremendous difficulties.

> The road is long
> full of traps
> The sun speaks of a time nourished by lost memory
> The salt returns to the grains of sand washed on the
>   banks
> With the migrations she leaves
> unaware of exile
> She filled her pockets with dreams
> her belt with images and music
> her blouse with rose petals
> She leaves as if shadows were coming back to life
> She navigates on drifting waves
> She does not see the death sentence
> mirror set upon the shore
> the bird smashing down upon the rocks
> The other waits for her, leaning against a red tree
> She calls, calls for reconciliation
> face turned toward the Milky Way
> syllables transforming rupture
> into harmonious song
> There is in her gestures so much love and pardon
> so much silence to fill the silences
> so much echo to find the sea
> She will be there to cradle the wounded bird
> stop the massacre by showering it with tears
> carry the child above the storms
> Her delicate determination traces a new land,
> land of forests with a multitude of butterflies

Her boat of peace takes in the abused
She slips pearls of tolerance in bouquets
She shows the crippled woman the route of the
    ringdove
She wraps her in silk and velvet
as her double
This is how all must begin anew

11

A sunny morning. A light dry desert wind. Aïda opens wide both doors and windows. She shakes out sheets, mattress and blankets, laying them over the gate. She is wearing her full, flowered skirt; wayward strands of hair halo her radiant face. She hums the refrain of a Tunisian song, the story of a love lost and recovered. Her quick then slow movements follow the rhythm of her breathing. She concentrates, her flexible body bends and straightens as if performing some secret ritual. She turns with the same ease as when she entered the sea, with her breasts naked to the wind, swimming towards the horizon, breathing in the open sea air. Her arms stretch forth, relax – a call to Gaïa. She is in harmony with the Earth, with the universe she loves, comforts and rebuilds to save it from destruction. Each of her movements conveys life. Hayate is fascinated once more by the expression of freedom emanating from her. Aïda, who has caught sight of her, exclaims:

'Come, we'll have coffee, then we'll take a walk in the sun. It's so nice outside!'

She leads her into the kitchen and heats the coffee.

'Where is your daughter?' enquires Hayate.

'Her father has taken her for the weekend. And Ahlame has already gone. She'll join us at the Club a little later.'

She pours the coffee into small cups, cuts the bread in slices, and spreads them with an appetising pomegranate jelly.

'Let's go out into the sunshine.'

They sit on the patio, on the low wall at right angles to that of the kitchen. Under their feet, a rug of tiny wild flowers has grown overnight. The scent of jasmine, violet and rose fills the garden. Aïda shakes her hair which shines in the light. She serves the coffee and the bread. She breathes deeply.

'It's still fairly cool, but the desert wind is going to bring the heat. We had best go to the souks early, before noon. In the Club it's always nice because the vaults keep it cool.'

Hayate looks at her with admiration.

'Where do you get your inner peace?' she says, sipping coffee.

'I look peaceful? What a nice thing to say. On the contrary, I feel like I'm always all keyed up. Especially lately, the quarrels among the women about the journal are tiring me out. After days spent teaching undisciplined noisy children, I have hardly any patience left. Sometimes I feel like abandoning everything. But I tell myself we've got to keep going, otherwise we leave room for fanaticism and regression. I'm taking yoga classes and they help me. I'm learning how to breathe and relax, to empty myself. Every morning, I go to the window and do my exercises. Sometimes I repeat them before going to bed. I feel in harmony with nature. That reconciles me with others.'

'This love of nature you have is obvious. It shows in your gestures and actions, and in the way you think.'

'In our countries, we don't take environmental problems seriously even though we should. If we do nothing to save Mother Nature, she won't forgive us; she'll disappear and we with her. Here people think that the land, the mountains, the flowers, the fish, the birds are things given to us for all time. They don't think about their situation. When they pillage, kill, destroy, and throw rubbish and waste just anywhere, they don't realise that Nature will avenge herself one day, that she has her limits, that we must take care of her, love her, protect her so that she agrees to stay with us and continues to produce the beautiful things she gives us – things we don't deserve.'

'It's not just a local problem. It's a global problem, which is much worse in the industrialised nations. Instead of concentrating all our efforts and capital on purifying the air, changing our means of transportation and finding gases that don't destroy, we develop weapons systems. We militarise and use Nature as if she were made for profit and selfish humanity. Instead of loving and respecting her, we end up destroying her.'

'Come on,' urges Aïda. 'Let's go to the souks before the midday heat.'

> Women walk in the light
> The path is scented with rose and jasmine
> Bougainvillaea covers the walls
> Crickets sing muezzins, temples and cathedrals
> At a bend in the road
> a dust cloud swells, carried off by the wind
> She goes toward the sea speaking of journeys
> Ahead there is war
> Brother has killed brother
> Other brothers avenge their brothers
> Olive, orange, apple trees are sacked
> pillaged and burned
> The sky is red with the blood of nights
> The city lies under a shroud of ash
> The Earth struggles under the weight of hatred
> Bends and does not recover
> Women, they walk still in the clear light
> Light they call forth with each step
> The patience to remake of the earth a garden
> The love to believe that love is possible
> On the dunes of their path stalks of broom have
>   sprung forth.

Around noon, the women accompany Rima to a small restaurant near the souks and the International Café. They order a Tunisian dish Hayate likes: squid with peas in a tomato and red pepper sauce. Rima is excited. She speaks rapidly about her activities at the newspaper, at committees and various organisations. She tells Hayate about all the difficulties she has had getting a reasonably priced apartment, in her own name, that she can occupy alone. If she hadn't had an important position with a newspaper, she would never have been able to rent a place. Her apartment is in a complex for government employees, but she lives in constant fear of being replaced by a man or a family, even though the men who use these apartments as second homes are in no danger of this. Hayate had not realised how hard it was for a woman to find a place to rent by herself in Tunis. Aïda mentions all that she went through after her divorce to stay in the house she currently occupies. This house is still in her ex-husband's name, which is not reassuring. She has tried in vain to put the house in her own name. She also lives with the fear that neighbours may force the owner to take back his house.

Rima outlines a current problem facing Arab women. The Arab League is seeking an extension of the code of civil rights common to all Arab countries in order to make conditions for women the same across the League. Most women believe that such an accord will mean a step backwards for Tunisian women. What can one expect from a country like Saudi Arabia concerning women's rights! Some women don't even want to talk about the problem or see the issue raised, saying they don't consider themselves to be Arab. Rima thinks that this refusal is serious; these women will be affected by the decisions made, whether they like it or not. They should discuss it in order to arrive at a common position among women to influence the League's decisions. But can women have an impact in the Arab League? Aren't they tearing each other apart precisely because they feel completely powerless and paralysed? Once more Hayate realises how much Fanon was correct in his analysis of the psychology of the oppressed.

Hayate asks Rima if she has written the article on Sana and Imane. She explains that she is in the process of writing it. More and more she feels the necessity of exposing another point of view because the newspapers are calling Sana a heroine. No one has raised the problem of violence implied by her act. All the articles glorify her as a martyr. No one has spoken of Imane. In her article, Rima has had the courage to formulate questions that need to be raised. She puts them to Sana as if she were still alive. She tells Sana she feels close to her and understands her, that she would have liked to talk with her at length before her suicide mission. At a certain point in time, she, too, would have been capable of throwing herself under a tank. She thought then that only violence

97

could resolve certain problems. Now she is no longer sure. She has noticed that violence calls forth more violence, that war brings about further war, that blood spilled increases bloodshed. She has realised that one must break this vicious circle with a position of active non-violence. She is now convinced that only the pacifistic attitude makes sense. She asks Sana if she would have participated in the peace march, had she been aware of it.

Aïda suggests to Rima that she make the distinction between resistance against Israel – the violence is then legitimate because of the aggression of the Zionist state – and conduct in the chaos of a civil war where pacifistic action can find its place. How can one fight against a war machine and a system ready to exterminate a people, in this case, the Palestinians? How could the Algerians, for example, have liberated themselves other than by an armed revolt? There are degrees of resistance; one must uncover them. The 'good intentions' that bring about a non-violent response risk demobilising individuals and the collective in the face of violent domination. How is non-violence effective? By what means does it change things, since change is the goal?

Hayate defends the idea that the question of non-violence is a pertinent one even in the case of foreign aggression, because the destructive power of modern weapons is such that disasters are of huge proportions, and it is almost always the poor, the deprived, that number among the greatest victims. She criticises military violence, such as that used by the PLO and certain Arab countries united materially and morally in unequal wars. These wars have led to the destruction of Lebanon, to the dispersal of its energy, manpower, and to the renewal of political tyranny in the entire Middle East. That is why one must ask the question: how can non-violence be effective today in Lebanon and in the world at large?

Aïda thinks that the peace march is an excellent idea. But weapons have kept it from happening; non-violent action has thus been squashed. The idea remains, but how can it be realised? By non-collaboration with the enemy, the occupier, of course. But a part of the population, men in particular, collaborate and seek to use outside forces to maintain their power inside, just as outside forces use them on the inside. So what can one do? Where is the answer?

For Rima, the peace march has meaning even if it seems to have failed. It can be taken up by all those who rise up against war and violence. It could unite the oppressed and dispossessed masses of the Earth in a common goal of salvation and life. Instead of using violence to obtain their rights – violence that turns against them once the new regime is in power, for violence feeds power and maintains it – they would find peaceful ways to demand justice. Once established, it would bring a real transformation of all the systems of power.

Hayate speaks of the line of demarcation dividing Beirut. This year, during a visit to Lebanon, she noticed that the line of demarcation had become a meeting place for an important part of the civilian population – women in particular who were saying no to the war. They had decided to cross Beirut at least two or three times a week to affirm their faith in unification and peace. They often did this under the bombs and gunfire of snipers, walking swiftly through the apocalyptic setting that the museum passage had become, smiling while crossing over to give each other courage, convinced that through this act, Lebanon would be reborn from its ashes. Such acts are truly visionary and constitute the strength capable of making changes happen, changes necessary to the survival of Lebanon and the world.

Hayate thanks Rima again for talking about this in her article. She thinks that Rima has a great deal of courage to write it, that she will no doubt be misunderstood by most of her Arab sisters. She admires Rima and supports her projects completely.

They have coffee at the International Café, then go to the Club. The women there seem tired, on edge and strained. They smoke non-stop. A debate has already begun. Jedla takes the floor:

'When Taher Haddad formulated his ideas of liberation for women, he was almost stoned for it. Now, Tunisians in power give "freedom" to women through paternalism. We do not live under a democratic regime. At the same time, certain groups – Islamists in particular – are doing all they can to rally men against the legal rights obtained through the personal status code, so that upon the death of Bourguiba, his reforms will be questioned.'

Hayate thinks of Taher Haddad. She read in a book by Souad Chater, *La Femme tunisienne: citoyenne ou sujet*, that he denounced polygamy and the veil and claimed the right to education for women. His ideas were called heretical – he was condemned and thrown out of the 'Zaïtouna' (the mosque and Islamic university) where he was teaching. That was in the 1920s. Haddad influenced the thoughts of succeeding generations; his programme of feminine emancipation was realised by President Bourguiba thirty years later. The reformed personal status code was passed in 1956. It sets the age of marriage at eighteen for girls, twenty for boys. Polygamy was outlawed, forced marriage abolished. A civil wedding was added to the religious ceremony. Unilateral repudiation was outlawed and replaced by a judiciary divorce with the right to joint custody of children. Adultery became punishable with the same sanctions for men as for women. Tunisia is the only Arab country to have a law for the adoption of children. But, emphasises Chater, the relationship of dominant/ dominated persists in the couple; no marriage is possible between a Muslim woman and a non-Muslim man, the woman continues to receive as her inheritance only half the amount due her brother, and the judicial body only includes eleven women. In 1972, there were 4,772 women teachers – 3,700 primary schoolteachers, 1,072 secondary schoolteachers and almost no women university profes- sors. To this day, no woman occupies the post of general manager or secretary general in public administration.

Chater's work had interested Hayate because it presented with much information and precision the situation of Tunisian women that she was trying to understand. This afternoon the debate is unstructured. Hayate has trouble following ideas taking off in all directions. Nora presents the problem of divorce:

'A woman has the right to ask for divorce, but when she has to live the life of a divorced woman, she realises how unequal her status is. If she keeps her children on half a salary and cannot find independent housing she is penalised by the divorce.'

Hala recognises the problem of women who work:

'The husband often considers a woman who works outside the house to be abandoning the conjugal home. And as the laws require the obedience of a woman to her husband, women find themselves slighted by the system. The concept of obedience should be replaced by mutual respect.'

'And don't forget about single and abandoned mothers,' adds Aïda. 'Certain laws are not respected. Judges apply the laws as they choose. We must meet and form associations to take responsibility for these problems. In order for women citizens to have the courage to make their needs known, they must feel supported. At the moment, women live out their condition in total isolation. Why is there no movement to protect women when it comes to these issues?'

'As for me, I demand the right to live my life differently,' proclaims Baya. 'There is too much hypocrisy in our way of life. We lack courage and we hide ourselves. I'd like to come out of hiding.'

'Shouldn't we speak of the right to be different?' continues Rima. 'This is the basis of every democratic society. Why not outline topics for this year's conference?'

'I think we should speak about our problems, about our present concerns,' says Zaïda.

'The Club is currently in a state of crisis,' states Nadya, 'and we aren't getting down to talking about the most essential problems. No one wants to ask the hard questions that would allow us to move forward.'

This remark annoys Rima who becomes impatient:

'Talk about crisis brings about crisis. We must approach these problems in a positive way; we can't give up before we start.'

'I agree with you, Rima,' says Zaïda. 'But if we just keep giving presentations without centering them on real problems, without getting to the vital issues, it just won't help us.'

'If the conference last year was a success,' Rima explains, 'it's because we asked essential questions. And not only did we have the participation of intellectuals, but we had women and men

101

from different walks of life and social classes. We managed to bring up the subject of sexuality, discuss it and link it to other topics.'

Ahlame who has just come in glowers around the room. She is wearing her large earrings in the shape of birds. Her hair looks blown about by the wind; there is a look of determination and provocation in her eyes. She ventures an ironic smile:

'You really believe that last year's conference on sexuality was a success? I thought it was a total fiasco. No one is ready to talk about sexuality in this country and even less in the Club. If only you knew how much I have been criticised and insulted and my name blackened by all kinds of rumours for what I've said – all just a way of ignoring, of avoiding the problems I had raised.'

'Don't be afraid of criticism,' says Rima, reassuringly. 'It proves that what you were talking about was, and still is, necessary. Maybe we should take up the theme of sexuality again precisely because it does raise so much controversy.'

'There is criticism and *criticism*,' intervenes Aïda. 'What Ahlame has gone through is intolerable and unacceptable. I don't think we are ready to discuss sexuality. I'd like to be able to put it all on the table, but I'm afraid for the future of the Club. I see it closing in upon itself more and more.'

'Club membership is diminishing, but that's no reason for us to be stop-gaps,' stresses Ahlame. 'Even if I don't find my place here, it's still due to the Club that I have come this far. The Club is like us. It's a distressed and cyclical person. If it has to die, it has to die. Right now, it exists. As far as I'm concerned, I'd like to take up the theme of sexuality again at the risk of being insulted once more, because there are so many questions we haven't discussed sufficiently – virginity, the relationship between mother, father, religion, lover, husband . . . We need at least one session for each of these topics.'

'I have some ideas for the conference,' interrupts Nadya. 'We should try to develop a pluralistic view of feminism – analyse different approaches that already exist and define ourselves with regard to them and our own experience. That is what will allow us to advance, to clarify our ideas on this movement.'

'I'm convinced that the subversive element of feminism leads to marginalisation,' says Aïda. 'Why not organise the conference around that question?'

'What interests me is understanding how women have come to feminism through political activity,' adds Nayla.

'What is feminism? There's a basic question,' states Nora. 'We are at a point which allows us to reflect on these things. The experience of the Club shows us that we have spontaneously chosen an informal path. We reject bureaucracy. Doesn't our "disorder" constitute an alternative?'

'I'd like to talk about my research on the image of women in society,' announces Samia. 'I've started to get people from different areas to speak to me. I spoke to one woman who told me she had refused to have intercourse with her husband for the last seven years unless he gave her money to feed the children. Feminist movements don't interest her. Bread is all important and she doesn't make the link between the two. In the statements I've collected, I find a lot of fear of fundamentalism. I'd like to talk about this. I have some extraordinary interviews I'd like to present at the conference.'

'It would be good for me to analyse how feminism and the Club are seen from the outside, by the members of my family, for instance,' says Dalale. 'The image we have created is often that we are disconnected from social reality. It's a question I'd like to discuss.'

'Concerning politics,' declares Rima, 'we continue to think in traditional ways, although last year's conference defined feminism with regard to power. Many of us attach too much importance to the subversive aspect. That bothers me because the subversive element is a reaction to something. I prefer an approach that has its own logic and doesn't define itself in negative terms. The left has always defined itself negatively, in reaction to something; I'd like to find another way. We must take up the issue of sexuality. It's essential to our progress. If we're afraid to approach this subject, our discussions will remain superficial.'

'We have to speak about feminism with regard to the rise of

fundamentalism,' says Hala. 'People are afraid to tackle this problem. There are also intellectual fundamentalists. They are the most dangerous. We've got to work on this topic.'

'Feminism with regard to the western world and Tunisian feminism compared to other countries of the Maghreb; where does our identity lie? I'd like to discuss this question,' declares Aïda.

Hayate thinks of an idea.

'If it interests you,' she proposes, after some hesitation, 'I could explain the different ideological currents of American feminism of the last ten years. That could be my contribution to the conference.'

At the word 'American', tension in the room rises. Hayate feels it mount, a clamour of protest follows. Hayate feels they are being aggressive towards her by their looks and partial statements indicating that the United States must not be brought up, is not a subject of discussion here. Hayate did not expect such a hostile reaction. She should not have proposed this subject. Not to mention that such a subject would demand a considerable amount of work, for she had never made such a comprehensive study. She notices, however, some signs of encouragement. But one of the women present attacks her with:

'What you are proposing has nothing to do with our subject of feminism in the Maghreb.'

'I thought it could be useful to place North African feminism in the context of world-wide feminist movements. American feminism being avant-garde in many of its aspects, it could be interesting to look at the different strands, to summarise them and to analyse how feminism in Tunisia resembles or differs from them. This would allow a response to the problem of specificity and identity – a response to the question: is feminism a western phenomenon exported to countries of the Third World? But I could talk about feminism in Lebanon if you prefer. That would be easier considering that I have just spent a year at the Institute for Women in Beirut and I have quite a bit of information.'

'I'd like you to speak about American feminism,' encourages Rima. 'I don't see why we always have to study our own societies.

We limit ourselves considerably with our approach. And we get stuck in our own view of things. We accept being objects of study without ever putting ourselves forward as subjects. We don't approach others informed and on equal terms.'

'Yes, yes, do speak to us about American feminism,' insist several women.

The meeting ends noisily and in disorder. Finally, the chosen theme for the conference is: 'Which feminism for the Maghreb?' This question will allow treatment of the different topics proposed – the questions of identity, language, fundamentalism and sexuality – and allow a new discourse on the condition of women to develop.

Hayate feels empty and uneasy. She regrets suggesting a subject that does not appear to interest the majority. Yet there are several women who spoke in favour of it and appreciate her suggestion. She decides to prepare her talk for them.

12

With her face pressed against the train window, Hayate watches the rolling seascape once more. Thick clouds of birds come together and disperse in long chains, in lace streamers, in shapes that stretch out, bunch together, move forward. The slow movement of the clouds responds to that of the birds. The still lagoon attracts them and pushes them from one horizon to the other. Hayate knows that the lagoon is going to be filled in and apartment buildings, shops, offices and skyscrapers will be built in its stead. Will she see this landscape the next time she returns to Tunis? Will the birds survive this destruction of their environment? She thinks of Lebanon tearing itself apart. On each trip there, she is struck by the devastation, the damage produced not only by the war but also by greed and disorderly, unaesthetic building that is destructive to nature and the environment.

The sea always plunges Hayate into nostalgic reverie. She dreams of departures and arrivals, of projects planned, those of her adolescence in front of this same sea, set against this same sky, the sky of her country. Everything seemed possible then, nothing could hold her back, the horizon would always be open to her. She was as yet unaware of life's bruises, wounds that sometimes do not scar but deepen, and whose marks never fade.

Hayate is depressed today. The conversations with the women, their behaviour towards her, all these discussions have exhausted her. It is strange, she tells herself, last year in Lebanon, despite the war, I felt a freedom, an opening of the spirit that I do not find here. Is it the multiplicity of faiths, of voices, of cultures, of languages, the mixing of ideas that gave to Lebanon its radiant face, free and emancipated, that inspired the old and popular expression, 'In Lebanon, we live *with* . . .'? Was it this climate of tolerance, this pluralism, this open-mindedness that had made it vulnerable? This region of the world was made intolerant through the destruction of ancient communities, grappling with a growing fanaticism born out of neglect and the anger of those excluded. Acceptance of the other, the joy of 'doing with' was beginning to disappear. Certain neighbouring countries, envious of this openness which had brought about prosperity and development, had done everything to close it down. For those who accept a system that refuses and wipes out the other, a pre-war Lebanon could be seen only as disturbing. Is that what had led to the tragedy, the fall into uncontrollable destruction, seemingly irrevocable chaos? Why had the Lebanese accepted this sinister adventure, this tragedy without end? Hayate asks herself these questions again and again.

> Like a violin which weeps before it grows silent
> Like a dove colliding with the archways of night
> Like water in search of its memory
> Like a spring which dies without summer
> Like a beach that calls a sea in hiding
> Like a bottomless well of inconsolable tears
> my country dances on barbed wire
> a child speaks to his dead brother
> another lines up fragments of bombshells
> a little girl sings, cradling a mangled doll
> They dream of leaving
> for a place where the trees never lose their leaves

Lost in her thoughts, Hayate did not realise that the train was already entering the station. She sees 'Salammbô' written in blue letters on the wall. She hurries along, walking quickly on the road shaded by trees. It is very warm. Approaching Nayla's house, she notices there is an unusual amount of activity. More cars than usual. People entering and leaving the house. They look sad and solemn, wearing dark clothing. Hayate senses something is wrong. She climbs the stairs quickly and finds herself face to face with Nayla's sister, her face red and swollen with tears.

'Do you know where Nayla is? We've been looking everywhere for her. Our mother has died.'

Hayate is shocked. Poor Nayla who almost never left her mother for fear that she would die in her absence, is at this very moment nowhere to be found. The young woman who takes care of the house comes up as well, with questions in her eyes. Hayate looks at them. She would like to be able to tell them where Nayla is, and at the same time is glad not to know. She understood how much Nayla needed to be alone. For twelve years her mother has been ill and during these last years, Nayla has had to take complete charge of her, day and night, feed her, take her to the bathroom, carry her from one room to another. During the last three years, Nayla had her mother sleep in her room so that she would not be so alone. Hayate had wondered where Nayla's father was during all this. She was appalled that he did not take care of his sick wife. If the situation had been reversed, if her father had been sick, her mother would have taken responsibility for him, as with a child. She looks at the two women.

'No, I don't know where Nayla is,' she replies. 'The day before yesterday she asked me to go to Tunis with some messages. She knew that her mother was doing badly and was afraid to leave her. What could have happened?'

She enters the mother's room. The place is filled with cigarette smoke, incense and candles. Women are seated everywhere. They fan themselves and wipe their foreheads. It is so hot! They fan the mother, too – a futile gesture. She lies on the bed, her face relaxed as Hayate has never seen it before. Nayla will be comforted to see her mother so serene. Fortunately, she has died in peace, thinks Hayate. This will help Nayla in her grief. She looks at the little thin face, her prominent cheekbones, the space between eye and eyebrow, refined features no longer strained by illness, her lips relaxed, calm hands resting on the white sheet.

> You leave in the love that she gave you
> You are leaving
> like a madonna in an evening softened by waiting

108

like an amazon shaking its wings for the last time
you opened your hands to receive the rose and the
lily-of-the-valley
She knows that there are mimosa and jasmine under
the moon
that she has offered you pages of life from her secret
garden
that a moment of love shared is worth a thousand
moments of solitude
But did you share that love burning on the dune
You whose life was no more than a breath
suspended on the branch
Did you see the violet ray dying with the sun?

Hayate sits down. How beautiful she must have been before her
illness, she thinks, observing the changes brought on by her death.
The face has resumed its classic shape, the traits of a Nefertiti.
Nayla had mentioned this, but Hayate thought it was the love and
admiration she held for her mother that made her so exceptional
in her eyes. Where did she go when she felt death approaching?

Some women enter the place and greet Nayla's sister. A dark,
brown-skinned woman with multicoloured scarves tied around
her forehead, wisps of hair visible and a tattooed waist, chin and
arms, comes in and sits on the floor. They bring her two rugs, one
mauve and the other red, a basket filled with little packets of
incense, soaps, eau-de-Cologne, heavy perfume, cotton, candles
and a large white shroud. She checks to see if she has everything
she needs. She then cuts the long, transparent white cloth into
pieces. Her bracelets jingle and ring with every movement.

Suddenly there are screams in the street. Hayate recognises
Nayla's voice. Her sister runs outside. Hayate would also like to
run out, but does not dare. She makes out bits of sentences, words
interrupted by sobbing. A long silence. Nayla comes in, supported
by her sister and several women. Her face is distorted, her eyes
full of tears. She stumbles on the landing, would have fallen if
friendly hands had not caught her. As soon as she sees her mother,

her expression brightens. Her grief lightens. She regains her spirit. Hayate knew it would happen. Her mother expresses such tranquillity in death, such calm and a softness so real that one can only accept this release, be happy that she is at rest.

Nayla approaches the bed and puts her hand on her mother's forehead, on her hair, on her lips and neck. She takes her hand and checks the pulse, incredulous. The hand falls cold and heavy. Nayla strokes her cheeks, covers her eyes with her hand, as if she had been there at the moment when they would be closed forever, as if it were she who had cradled her for the last time. She needs to carry out these actions to relieve her grief. She must follow these rites to resolve her suffering. Outlining the contours of her face, she bids her goodbye.

Then she collapses, prostrate, at the foot of the bed. Hayate comes near and takes her hand. Nayla gives a flicker of a smile upon seeing her:

'You are here? Since when?'

'I've just arrived. Where were you?'

'I went to a meeting of the National Union for Tunisian Women. Imagine! I took my mother's temperature, which was normal – better than the last few days. She seemed to be better. Her body cooler. She seemed calmer, even restful. I came to the conclusion that she was improving and I left for the meeting. I needed to get out for a short while. If I had thought for a second that she was close to the end . . . If I had known . . .'

Nayla begins to cry again. A woman brings her orange flower water, reputed to have a calming effect. Hayate continues to squeeze her hand and sit close to her. Another woman offers her a cigarette. Nayla composes herself, accepts and lights it. She notices the woman cutting the shroud. Hayate observes the coming and going of the scissors, the suppleness of her fingers measuring the cloth, aligning the pieces. All of the women watch the details of this rite. All of these women surround Nayla and the mother who no longer needs their help. Hayate feels out of place. She gets up, kisses Nayla and says goodbye to Nayla's sister and the housekeeper.

As she is leaving, she notices the men in the neighbouring room. So, even at the time of death, men and women are separated, sighs Hayate. Do they have their rituals as well? What are they like? She is tempted to go in, to watch; 'curiosity will be the end of you,' her father had told her. This phrase, which comes back to her while watching the men of her own culture, brings back taboos, restrictions, everything she has tried to overcome. How can she live differently? How does one get rid of shackles and chains? How can one give the bird an azure sky? How does one regain the sea?

She moves away, quickly going down the staircase. She walks along by the sea, unmoving under the strong sun. She can hardly picture this place, inaccessible in the summer, according to what someone has told her, invaded by city dwellers coming to swim and find some respite from the heat. There is such emptiness, such calm at this time of year. Most of the houses are unoccupied. There are many villas under construction. There are deserted work sites. In a few years, there will be no space left, no trees, no nature. Everything will be invaded by buildings, concrete. At this hour, there are only cats picking through refuse.

She returns to her house. The telephone is still out of order. She makes a cup of coffee and sits at her desk. She looks out at the sea glistening with shades of silver and gold, gradually taking on red and violet rays with the approach of night.

She thinks about what Nayla and Ahlame have told her, about the malicious gossip and accusations of which she is the object. Her fears have been confirmed. What can she do? Confront those who sling mud at her? Ask for explanations? She does not know them well enough to do so. There is one of them, however, she knows and to whom she should speak – Samia. Samia has been involved in the rumours. She must give an explanation; one cannot let things go without speaking up, just because it is easier to ignore them than to confront them. She must make an appeal to her sense of justice and fairness, ask her the reasons for this defamation of character. Solidarity among women, it has to exist! Cultivate it so that it lives; she must not let these misunderstandings accumulate.

Hayate wants to know what is happening, to get to the bottom of things. Not so long ago, Samia was a friend despite her cool and reserved manner. What could have happened? Not so long ago, they had organised a large party for Rima's birthday. They had gone to the market all three of them and had done the cooking together. Hayate had borrowed the embassy house that had been entrusted to her. A crowd of people had come. They had eaten, drunk, danced, sung songs. They had laughed and enjoyed themselves. A few had become ill, not used to drinking wine, alcohol. There were some disagreeable exchanges among the guests. But all in all, the party was a success. Rima was so happy to have had a celebration. The women had assured Hayate that it had been a long time since they had relaxed and enjoyed themselves to that extent.

Yet the ill feelings must stem from that evening. Suddenly Hayate makes the connection: a house from the American embassy ... almost a palace! – while most of the women lived in fairly modest houses – violently anti-American reactions of most of the women, the accusations of working for the CIA. Everything is becoming clear. In the minds of certain women, she could only allow herself such luxury because she is paid for information passed to the American secret service. She only invited them in order to obtain more information. One must really have a Manichean, calculating mind to see everything in such drastic terms and draw such extreme conclusions.

But why those rumours of a sexual nature? She has still not discovered the key to the puzzle. Ahlame had analysed it well. It is jealousy mixed with guilt, the fear of what a person desires and rejects at the same time, feelings that someone projects upon another out of envy, despair, unhealthy living, frustrated sexuality. During the evening, some of the women had drunk too much, felt out of sorts and had gone upstairs to lie down. She saw some of the couples kissing. The dances at the end of the evening were quite wild, but nothing shocking or uncouth. And even if there had been more, why the pettiness?

All of a sudden, Hayate becomes angry. She had thought she

was doing a nice thing by agreeing to borrow this place, which was ideal for a party. She wanted to please Rima, whom she liked very much. She never should have offered a house that was not her own. What right did she have to borrow that house? She was only a guest, taking care of the cats of an American woman from the embassy until her return. Only long enough to find lodging. All this nonsense should teach her a lesson – wanting to help others and being paid back with slander! She was punished for her generosity with things that she didn't even own!

But this reasoning is also a masochistic simplification, a return to the morality of her childhood. After all, an embassy house belongs to everyone. It is no more the property of this woman than of the Tunisian people. Why not use it? Why not bring pleasure to her friends, those who love and understand her? Why deprive some of them of a pleasure because of the narrow-mindedness and distorted morality of others? And why should she feel guilty now? Is there a mistake to uncover in every misfortune? Where does the fault lie?

Suddenly, she understands the situation. During the party, there is an unravelling, a letting go of repressed desire, an unleashing of instincts, a collective reversal of the usual behavior. The party is a kind of hadra, or an inverse hadra. The hadra has the power to purify and heal; the pleasure of the party produces a guilt reaction – the remorse of having given oneself over to pleasure. The hadra reinforces the hierarchy of the sexes, traditional morality, the organisation of society and of sexual roles. The party breaks taboos and norms, is an expression of rebellion, while the hadra controls insubordination.

Anti-Americanism is also the idea of the great devil – the Manichean beast of the Apocalypse. Manicheism says that evil is in the Other and that one must fight it; that one must rid the self of it at any price in order for Goodness and Justice to triumph. To reject this idea because it leads to violence and war is to accept that evil also resides inside oneself – an intolerable idea that few people are capable of admitting. Violence against the other person is justifiable; it proves that one is good, that one has nothing to do

113

with evil. Violence is linked to fear, fear of the other, but also fear of oneself, of the evil within the self, fear of having to admit it and live with it.

Hayate realises that it is not surprising that her ideas of non-violence and change in human relationships stir up so much distrust, rejection, bitterness and hatred. It is so much easier to put responsibility on others, to see evil in them, to attribute all faults to them, so as not to have to transform oneself. It is more reassuring to believe that one holds truth and justice than to seek to understand the other – the one who is different. To admit that evil is also in oneself is to admit that evil is perhaps not evil. Evil is also that which is abnormal, that which does not concern everyone. The universal, in one sense, cannot be evil.

She is frustrated with her telephone still being out of order. She would really like to talk to Aïda, to ask her advice, to hear the voice of a friend, to be reassured in her distress. She thinks of the death of Nayla's mother, which adds to her depression. Death is a part of oneself that dies in others, everything one has projected on to that other person. Nayla must be suffering a lot right now; she had given so much to her mother, she had repressed her own anguish while taking care of her. And yet this death is also a release. It will allow Nayla to free herself, to live elsewhere if she wants, to discover who she is, far from the family circle. Hayate is convinced that she needs this to happen in order to find herself, to develop. And also, she keeps telling herself, she must be happy to see her mother depart in peace, without suffering.

> When the flame has extinguished itself in cool
>   morning
> you will travel further than the river of lost memory
> you will go
> your gaze lost in dreams
> hair flashing with a thousand rays
> forehead pale, turned upward
> you will go
> you do not know hatred and vengeance

you have always given without measure
your hands are still open to the pages of your life
already closed
you have long sought a love without doors
a boat without anchors
a people without boundaries
you leave in the time of silences
kneeling on a flowering earth
this will be your shining night of tenderness

13

At her window that looks out towards the sea, Hayate is hunched over pages covered with a round, sensual, tormented script. She is trying to write about the events, feelings, questions, frustrations and the moments of happiness she has just lived through. She is amazed that so many things have happened so rapidly during these last few days. All of a sudden she realises that she had idealised the women, their journal and their movement, and that these women had projected their own frustrations on to her and also onto themselves. A play of mirrors. Ideas formulated from reflections of the other. A picture based on what one carries inside.

Should she be more vigilant, not open up except to those in whom she has total confidence, keep her thoughts to herself, her secret garden only for true friends? This is a lesson life has already taught her. Why was she not more careful? Isn't caution something one gets caught up in, a perversion that prevents you from seeing and understanding, from grasping problems and situations?

She thought she had found the place of her fulfilment – a place for dialogue and solidarity among women, a centre for new growth in the Arab world, a culture that drew her in profoundly. She was persuaded that in this place would appear answers to the chaos in which her country and her region of the world seemed to be floundering. The events of the last few days had shown her the cracks, the insurmountable difficulties, the trenches that women (and men) dig between each other because they are afraid of understanding, afraid of opening up, loving, accepting one another, afraid of living differently.

There are also economic factors which play a decisive role in all of these questions. They are as urgent as the issue of sexuality, even if the economic factor has been studied in greater detail along with the political and the cultural. How can one have a true dialogue with people who are struggling with insurmountable material difficulties? How can one build lines of communication? And how can nations expect to understand other nations that they have colonised and which they continue to dominate materially, culturally, politically, psychologically and economically?

Even if turning the United States into the Arch-Satan shows a limited, over-simplistic way of seeing the world, politics, human beings, life, they are still present with their hegemony, their political clout. Hayate must face these questions; she must try to understand and get to the bottom of things, find answers. The idea of a great demon is a childish response which reassures people and comforts them in their pettiness, with their life that otherwise would be stifling. It separates them from the complexity of things, from understanding others and differences, from a subtler, pluralistic view. It prevents them from seeing the whole picture. But it is a logical reaction, part of the unhappy lot of the have-nots and dispossessed who turn inward because life is too painful. Lacking essential things, they withdraw with the idea of a reward after death if they practise a moral code for good against evil. They console themselves this way with the idea that they are not capable of domination! By creating the great demon, they are no longer accomplices to the domination; they can then continue this complicity, this pettiness.

To create a great demon is a way to obtain a clear conscience. The appetite for material things, the desire to consume brings with it a feeling of guilt. One is unhappy because of one's relationship to desire, attraction and rejection all at once which divides people. For example, the attraction of free sexuality gives birth to a bad conscience. To say that evil is external to the self is to say that one has not been tempted. To dissolve the great demon is to enter into the complexity of moralism. Moralism is linked to temptation; the forbidden creates temptation, anguish and fear of freedom.

How could Hayate expect to communicate with women that see her with an American research grant, the U.S. the most detested and envied country in the world, a country which is the main factor and symbol of world domination? In their eyes, what could she have come to study and how will she use this information?

And yet with Aïda communication is possible and profound. Aïda is the centre of everything. Her house is open to women and the world. Aïda is also above all this. Material considerations, petty and calculated to hurt others, are alien to her relationship to life. Born in another country and under different conditions, Aïda would have been just the same: generous, big-hearted, welcoming, in perfect harmony with nature and the earth. Rima, Halima, Ahlame, Hala, Sihame and Afafe all share this quality of soul. With them, faithful and sincere relationships, communication about essential things, is also possible. Fortunately people such as her exist everywhere in the world, sighs Hayate. They (men and women) are the hope of the world.

Lost in her thoughts, she did not hear the gate to the garden open. Abruptly, the door to the house is shaken. She runs to see who could be in such a hurry that they haven't taken the time to announce themselves. It must be someone who has the key to the gate. In fact, it is the landlord with two workers:

'We have come to repair your telephone.'

'Come in, come in,' says Hayate, shocked by the lack of respect for her privacy, but happy they have come to fix the telephone.

The three men come inside the house. The two workers check the wires and the telephone. The landlord examines the house and Hayate with a look that makes her ill at ease.

'Would you like a cup of coffee or something cool to drink?' she asks to hide her discomfort and be hospitable in spite of her wish to see them leave.

'A glass of cool water,' request the workers, sweating from the heat.

Hayate goes to the refrigerator. She has no ice because the freezer is out of order, but she does not want to complain about it in order to avoid being invaded again, stared at, bothered. She offers the water. The workers drink avidly. They discover what has gone wrong and go back to work. They repair one of the exterior wires broken during the fury of the storm, the night when

118

the wind was blowing so fiercely. They check that everything is in place and call the operator. The telephone works!

Hayate thanks them and accompanies them to the door. She runs to the phone and calls Aïda, who does not reply. At this hour, she is teaching. Suddenly she is conscious of a presence in the room. She turns around, cold with terror. It is the landlord.

'Would you care to make me the cup of coffee you offered before?'

Taken aback, she stutters:

'I don't have the time. I have to leave for a meeting.'

She sees that he has leaned up against the living room door, the only door to the outside. He studies her with a perverted gaze that freezes her blood. What is she to do? She could cry out for hours; no one would hear her – the house is isolated, especially at this time of year when all of the surrounding houses are empty. She goes towards the door and mumbles:

'Oh well! I'll make you the coffee.'

He grabs her wrists.

'It doesn't matter. You don't have time. But get undressed, just for a moment. I want to see your body.'

Now he is using the familiar form of French address, 'tu', with her. She tries to get away, but the more she struggles, the more he presses his large fingers into her arm. Amazed by the calm emanating from her despite the fear she feels, she speaks to him in Arabic:

'So this is how Tunisian men behave? Aren't you ashamed? Would you treat your sister this way?'

She hopes to appeal to his sense of honour, his reputation as an Arab male, but his grip on her remains tight. Surprised by her tirade in Lebanese Arabic, he replies, this time in Tunisian Arabic:

'Why? Are the Lebanese different? We are westernised now.'

Then he continues in French:

'You've got a beautiful body. You are making me crazy. I want to suck you. I want to see it.'

He begs her. He resembles a pig with his fat body, his thick hands, his wide neck, sagging eyes, bloated cheeks and huge

119

stomach. The sweat is beading on his forehead, his pupils are dilated with greed.

Hayate is seized with rage. Never before has she felt herself so capable of violence. She would kick him in the head or groin if she knew the technique. She fears the worst, feels incapable of going as far as she must in her rage. Besides, he is certainly stronger than she is. He could easily rape her, kill her even, and wash his hands of it. She should keep a cool head, try to trick him with a ruse instead.

She attempts to escape once again.

'It is very warm,' she declares, surprised by the firmness of her tone despite her terror. 'I'll show you my body, but let me breathe. And anyway, close the curtains. The neighbours might see us.'

It is the best suggestion that occurs to her. He runs to the window to close the curtains. She throws herself towards the door, opens it and runs into the kitchen. Fortunately, the entrance is not locked. She rushes into the garden, her strength doubled by her fear. The landlord follows. She turns around and yells at him:

'Leave this house immediately or I'll call the police.'

'Don't get so worked up. I'm leaving. Why are you so mean? I only wanted to see your body. You really don't want to show it to me?'

'I told you to leave immediately.'

She's reached the end of her patience, the limit of what her nerves can stand. She indicates the gate:

'Leave the premises. Go, leave, or I'll get the neighbours out.'

She knows that at least behind the house, on the other side of the street, there is a bakery that should be open at this time of the day. There is also a lifeguard/security guard that passes by from time to time. The landlord should know this. He is no longer sure of himself. He goes off, muttering:

'Nervous, cruel woman . . .'

Hayate's heart is beating as if it would burst. Her body is shaking. A cold sweat breaks out on her forehead. She waits to see if he has really left the place. She watches his car pull away, waits to hear the engine in the distance, then goes back inside to make a call. But who can she call? At this hour most of her friends are at work, and how could they help her? Should she alert the police? Where would she find the number and what would she say? There is only one possible alternative: to call the American embassy, the administrator of a research grant she has obtained for the year. Trembling, she dials the number and asks for the cultural attaché.

'What's wrong? Your voice is barely recognisable. You seem shaken up.'

In a few words and stopping to breathe deeply several times, she explains what has just occurred.

'I'm particularly afraid that he might return. I don't feel safe.'

'We'll send out the Tunisian embassy police right away. Pack your bags, we'll send someone to help you move. You mustn't stay there alone. We'll find a place for you to sleep tonight.'

She recognises American efficiency. She thanks the attaché, hangs up and goes from one side of the room to the other. She wanders around without knowing what to do or where to start. It makes her sad to leave this house with the garden and the view of the sea that she adores. And she is now adjusted to it, there is a rhythm in her work and she has organised herself for what is left to accomplish. It upsets her to have to change.

She notices that she is shivering despite the heat and that she has spent almost half an hour wandering aimlessly from one end of the house to the other. If only she could speak to Aïda, she would feel better. She is not sure any more that she did the right thing by speaking to the embassy. She does not want to be labelled with what the United States represents in Tunis: imperialism and domination/oppression. What she has just discovered recently is that she is criticised and slandered because she teaches in the US and obtained a research grant from there. This made her vulnerable and upset. She would have preferred to turn to someone else. But who should she contact? What else can she do? Suddenly the telephone rings. It is the cultural attaché.

'Is everything all right? Have you packed your bags? We're sending over a driver. He'll be there in less than an hour. We have found a place for you to stay: a member of the embassy staff is leaving and would like someone to look after the house. You can stay there until the end of your time here.'

'Could you give me more time to pack? I won't have finished within the hour.'

'How much time do you need?'

'About three hours.'

'OK. We'll send a car in three hours. The embassy police would like you to make a statement at the station when you like. In the meantime, call us if there is any problem.'

'Thank you, thank you.'

She is touched by the rapidity and solicitude of the attaché and at the same time she is terribly worried about the idea of having to go to the police station to make a statement. For the moment, she must sort out everything and tidy up. Ever since the landlord's visit, she feels as if she is being pulled over a precipice, into a fearful machine. She was so happy in this house which she had organised for her stay, to work in and receive friends.

She feels paralysed, incapable of putting her things in boxes, incapable of seeing what she must take or leave behind. It must be the aftermath of fright, this feeling of being nailed to the floor. She must take hold of herself. She has only to throw things pell mell into suitcases or boxes. Fortunately she has not thrown away some boxes brought from the embassy store where she had gone shopping the week before. If she concentrates on this move, she will not think about her fright, her anxieties, the fear which grips her when she remembers the obscene look of the landlord, with his large, vicious hands. In order to finish in three hours, she must get going without delay.

She piles all her clothes into suitcases and her papers and books into boxes. She stuffs preserves and other products into large bags and puts the perishable food into plastic carriers. Fortunately, she has not bought too much food lately! She moves things, transfers them, puts them in cases and decants them; she organises things and moves them again, circulating from one place to another without being able to fix her attention on any one thing or any one place. She goes from a box to a suitcase, from a case to a bag, from a cardboard box to a plastic bag, from the kitchen to the bathroom, from the chest in her bedroom to the refrigerator. She goes to such lengths that she forgets her fear. Her confusion about packing masks her terror, her panic.

She stops for a moment and sees that she has almost finished, that she is sweating profusely and that her three hours are almost up. She flies into the shower – her last shower in this little house to which she is so attached. She remembers the impressions she had upon her arrival: the smell of the sea on the walls, water flowing everywhere and even under the door, the taste of salt on her skin, magnolia soap, the water that stops and starts unpredictably, the damp in blankets and cushions, her hair made curly by the sea breeze, the lily-of-the-valley scent she found in a shop that deodorises the bath and sink.

She dries quickly and puts on clean clothes. She feels calmer and more relaxed. She sees that she has forgotten some things in her haste. She packs some of them . . . too bad about the rest! She has done well in such a short time.

She hears a car horn and sees the embassy car from the window. She runs to open the door. The chauffeur bustles about, helping her move. In a few minutes, all her things are in the car. The place feels empty and abandoned. A few boxes and things are scattered here and there as if to mark her absence and departure. Hayate finds it hard to wrench herself away from this place which has sheltered her and made her love the country, this house which has helped her to endure her nostalgia for Lebanon, which she's missed so much. She sighs and takes a final look around to see if she has left anything essential. She closes and locks the door, looks one last time at the sea with its red and green hues that she will never again see from this vantage point. She climbs into the car. The driver asks her if she has forgotten anything, and drives away.

Hayate is seized with melancholy, with the sadness of a departure she did not want and could hardly have imagined just a few hours before. This forced departure reminds her of other departures, in particular the one which brought her to Tunisia. She was supposed to be in Lebanon this year; her research and teaching

123

grant had been renewed. The American Embassy had been bombed, so they had forbidden her to travel to Lebanon. They had sent her to Tunisia. In the beginning, she felt terribly frustrated at not being able to return to a country she loved so much. Then she became attached to Tunisia, thanks to this house by the sea. She could take long walks along the coast and discover the Punic harbours, the heritage of the Phoenician civilisation, and therefore a bit of her own, since Lebanon was the cradle of the Phoenician people. She could gather wild flowers and fill the house with them and rediscover the Mediterranean sky, the starry nights and enchanting moons of her own country. All of this had been taken away from her again.

She feels tears well up in her eyes. She turns her head to the window so that the driver does not notice them. Does he suspect anything? What did they say to him at the embassy? She had often been surprised at the offhand way in which the American staff spoke to the Tunisian staff at the embassy. The Americans treated them with disdain and superiority. Quite obviously the Tunisian people represented the epitome of foreignness. They were considered non-human and used for subordinate tasks, underestimated, regarded as 'underdeveloped', retarded, backward. She is once again annoyed to be associated with this kind of 'racism'. But is it not more a question of class than of race or country? She has seen rich Tunisians treat their own staff the same way. One could hope that a people with a long democratic tradition would have learned to behave better, in a more egalitarian and just way.

As usual, Hayate is idealising, seeing others as she would like them to be. She projects on to them what she feels inside, which rarely corresponds to reality. However, she reassures herself, with Aïda she is not projecting anything. Aïda is her soul sister. This is why they understand each other so well. They see in each other what they admire and respect. And they discover what they lack, what they would like to be. More than this enriching and exalting mirror, it is the other – the same and yet different – which adds to the relationship.

Hayate had noticed that when speaking English among themselves, certain Americans at the embassy imagined, or wanted to think, that the Tunisians who drove their cars or worked in their gardens or houses did not understand their slang, their play on words, their sarcasm. And that even if they did grasp the meaning, they just had to take it, to swallow the criticism and bend down before the 'great' American culture, the most advanced, the most civilised country. Hayate was deeply shocked and hurt by this attitude. She knew that the Tunisians understood perfectly well everything that was said, that they feigned ignorance, that barriers of misunderstanding and hatred were building up right in front of her eyes. Once Hayate had even taken the risk of making a remark in Arabic to a driver to express her unhappiness with what was said. The driver had not reacted to the comment. Conscious of his class and his place, he had preferred to keep silent. Afterwards she had noticed that he was particularly attentive and nice to her.

Upon arriving in Tunis, the driver takes a familiar road.

'Are we going to El-Menzeh?' Hayate asks.

'Yes, didn't you know?'

'No, they just told me I'd be moving into a house, without telling me where. I know El-Menzeh well, I've already stayed there. Among other things, I looked after the cats and house of Madame Doolittle; it's a fabulous palace.'

'The house you'll be in is smaller, but it's very beautiful.'

'Will there be a garden full of fruit trees and flowers, too?'

'The garden is much smaller. There are flowers, but no fruit trees.'

'That's a shame, I used to love picking the oranges and lemons and pressing them for fruit juice in the morning.'

'You'll see, this house is very nice.'

He stops in front of a two-storey villa made of slabs of cut stone. A caretaker comes to open the gate and helps them to bring bags, boxes and suitcases inside. She thanks them and gives them a few dinars she has on her. She closes the door and examines the place. It is spacious and comfortable. The furniture is American taste. Hayate learned that the embassy imports everything from

125

the U.S. The furniture is massive and heavy, comfortable and practical, but totally lacks the aesthetic quality and life necessary to create an ambience. In the kitchen, there is the enormous American refrigerator with its enormous freezer and the enormous stove with its pilot lights – a useless waste of gas in this country where most people live without necessities and do not even have the equivalent of gas consumed by pilot lights or any appliance to cook with. This lodging is reduced to consumer goods! All of this disgusts her. Why did she agree to come here? But did she have a choice?

She feels as if she is in a box, in a closed, square place. She already misses the view of the sea. She climbs on to the roof, hoping to glimpse it, but she sees only the hills of El-Menzeh, and villas everywhere. She climbs down and pours a glass of ice water. She is terribly thirsty.

She goes to the telephone and calls Aïda. She is there! She tells her in a few words what has just happened. Aïda asks why she did not move to her place. She would have been so happy to have her. Hayate had not thought of it, and even if the idea had crossed her mind, she would have been afraid of disturbing her; and in any case she could not reach her before the move. Aïda insists that she never disturbs her, that they could have worked together and encouraged one another. She can still come over if she wants – her house is open to her at all hours of the day and night. Hayate is touched. She feels the close friendship that Aïda has for her. She is so generous she would give the little that she has. Hayate knows that her space is limited and that she fights against great material and moral difficulties. She tells her to come with her daughter to the embassy house. This villa is immense, they could live together easily and benefit from the comfort.

Then she asks if she should go to the police station to file a report. Aïda does not know. It is a difficult question. They must think about it, not act too quickly. Aïda seems tired. She replies in monosyllables. She has had an exhausting day with her undisciplined students, and with futile arguments about the journal. Hayate is also worn out. The emotions of the day have beaten her down. She has only one desire – to go to bed and forget. They will call each other the next day. Hayate swallows a tranquilliser to help her sleep.

> In my country of magic, of the inextricable
> I spoke of spring when it was winter
> I drew a poppy in the massacre
> I imagined a rainbow in place of the cyclone
> I wanted to throw the windows wide open to the
> light
> The sun was veiled with the dust of the bombs'
> ashes
> They took the old woman
> the one who had written so much about Lebanon
> and women
> the one whose children's books enchant
> tell a story of love and sharing
> draw rivers of butterflies and violets
> the one who worked day and night for renewal
> for reconciliation
> the one who carried the hope of a Lebanon united
> and at peace
> They tied her to the road with other old ones
> a screen of anger and horror
> so that the tanks of the enemy brother
> would not pass through
> But the tanks passed
> . . .
> I cry now all the tears of the earth

14

A ringing telephone awakens Hayate, who jumps from the bed, shocked to find herself in an unfamiliar place. Then she remembers leaving the house at the sea she loved so much. What time could it be, who could be calling? She answers . . . a friendly voice, Afafe, a young Arab scholar.

'Hello, Hayate, how are you? I've just heard about all the terrible things that have happened.'

'Really? How do you know?'

'Tunis is small – news travels fast. The priest at the Institute of Arab Literature was informed and he told me. He feels badly for you and would like to visit so that you don't feel alone. We could come together perhaps. What are you going to do?'

'I don't know. I feel tired, quite worn out. The embassy advised me to register a complaint at the police station; I wonder if that's a good idea. What do you think?'

'You must go. It's not an easy thing to do but it's essential. If you don't go, people will question your story.'

'If I decide to go, it will be mostly for other women. I tell myself that if I don't have the courage to go to the police, then this man or others like him will think that whenever they like, they can frighten, intimidate, rape, and even kill women if the fancy takes them.'

'You're right. If you want, I'll go with you.'

'Really? Would you come with me? I'm so touched. I didn't have the courage to go alone, but if you come along, that will give me the strength I need.'

'I have my car. I'll come and get you as soon as you like.'

'Give me time to wash and get dressed. What time is it?'

'It's 8:30. I'll be at your house in an hour if that's all right.'

'Fine. Thanks so much.'

Hayate is touched by Afafe's call, by her solicitude, her spirit of solidarity. Afafe has spoken to her about her life, great difficulties that have made her sensitive to others' pain. Hayate knew just how much the priest at the Institute had helped her to achieve when everything was crumbling around her. Hurt so many times, especially by men, Afafe is thirsty for liberty, absolutes, justice. The priest – her friend – personifies the values she holds dear. He lives them, more or less successfully, but he lives them. He is genuine with himself and others. Afafe needs this role model. And also, unlike other men, the priest does not threaten her sexually. She can laugh with him, speak openly, count on him as a friend, and even confide in him without fear of a misunderstood gesture or breach of confidence.

Hayate makes a cup of coffee and runs a bath. In this house everything works, everything seems new and perfectly clean. The telephone rings again. It is the cultural attaché. He asks if she has had a good night. She thanks him. He wants to know what she intends to do about the police. She tells him that she is going to the station this morning with a Tunisian woman friend. He will send the Tunisian embassy police to help her; the police station is in Carthage, near Salammbô. Hayate thanks him and hangs up. Once again she feels dragged into a chain of events over which she has no control.

She has just finished dressing when the doorbell rings. It is Afafe, with her broad smile and comforting presence.

'I persuaded my brother to come with us. You never know. We might need a man in this kind of situation.'

'The embassy has also sent their police to help us.'

'Excellent! They will never think of taking this lightly with such chaperones. Are you ready? Let's go.'

Hayate closes the door, says hello to the caretaker, and climbs into Afafe's little red car. Her brother is seated in the back. He smiles broadly at her. The brother and sister have the same smile, thinks Hayate. She feels confident with these two people she likens to wild, sympathetic birds. In the car, Afafe puts on a tape of Joan Baez. The heat is stifling and she opens the windows wide. She begins to drive in a dizzying fashion. She lights a cigarette and offers one to Hayate and her brother. She raises the volume of the music and sings the refrains she knows by heart. The voice of Joan Baez is warm and sensual, surprising under these circumstances:

> For I'll be damned, here comes your ghost again
> But it's not unusual
> It's just that the moon is right and you happen to
>   call
> And here I sit, and on the telephone
> Hearing a voice I'd known
> . . .
> I remember your eyes were bluer than lavender
> My poetry was lousy you said
> . . .
> We both know what memories can bring
> They bring diamonds and rust
> . . .
> The answer my friend is blowing in the wind
> The answer is blowing in the wind
> How many deaths will it take till we know
> That too many people have died
> . . .
> The answer is blowing in the wind.

The cassette is over, Afafe puts in another and continues to sing. Hayate is fascinated, enchanted by the music and the lyrics. Music has a mystical, magical power, she thinks once again. She forgets her fear, her apprehension of a confrontation with the police.

> Brezhnev took Afghanistan, Begin took Beirut
> Galtieri took the Union Jack, and Maggie over lunch
>   one day
> Took a cruiser with all hands
> Apparently to make him give it back
> . . .

> I know I'll never know war
> And if I ever do the glimpse will be short
> Fireball in the sky
> No front line battle cries can be heard
> And the button is pushed by a soul that's been
>   bought
> I'll know no war
> . . .
> Give peace a chance
> Give peace a chance
> . . .

For the first time since she has been in Tunisia, Hayate meets someone who is familiar with American revolutionary music. A pleasant surprise which plunges her into an America she misses. Usually in Tunisia, political music, played on the radio or by women, is French. The radio plays a lot of American rock, sometimes jazz, but rarely these peace songs which are touching and go straight to the heart and make people sensitive to world issues.

'Where did you find this music that no one here seems to know?' asks Hayate.

'In general, Tunisians prefer Arab music, French songs or American rock. It's a shame; they are missing so much. Too bad for them! Maybe it's a question of language. With rock, they don't have to think about the lyrics which are covered up by the rhythm. In order to understand and appreciate peace songs, you need a smattering of English. But these cassettes, you can find them and buy them here.'

Afafe looks at her with her beautiful smile and puts in another cassette. This time it is Bob Dylan who evokes freedom in his raucous and haunting voice.

The music shortened the trip and made her less anxious; they arrive in Carthage. The police station is easy to find. Afafe parks her car right in front of the building, next to a dumbfounded security guard. She gets out, accompanied by Afafe's brother. The embassy police, who were waiting in an embassy car, approach them.

They enter together. Hayate makes her statement. In the beginning, only one police officer is present, taking notes, then others arrive to ask more questions. A group forms. It's as if all of the building's inhabitants, having learned of the show, had passed the word to come attend the vaudeville act. They are speaking Tunisian Arabic that Hayate does not always understand. Fortunately, Afafe is there to help her, to translate and above all to support her. Each time Hayate looks her way, she loses her fear and manages to express herself. Afafe will tell her afterwards that she had to hold herself back from becoming annoyed or bursting out laughing; what the officers were saying was often vulgar and ridiculous. They were using Tunisian swear words; wanting to ask questions which showed what voyeurs they were, and Afafe told them that these questions were useless and indecent.

Finally, they ask Hayate what she expects from her statement. She responds naively that she hopes that the man will not do this again, and will understand that the act he has committed will not be tolerated, and that he should repent and change his attitude and the way he acts around women.

Afafe will tell her later that the policemen were surprised by this response; they thought she had come to the police station to receive some financial compensation. Without a doubt, they wouldn't have been more surprised had she asked for the moon! To want such a man to change – what a delusion!

They leave the station, thank the embassy police and go back to their car and set off. Hayate is relieved. She offers to buy them a pizza in a local restaurant. Afafe has very little time – she has to take an exam the next day and has not yet studied for it. Once more Hayate is touched by her thoughtfulness, her concern for others; she took the time to accompany her even though she had so much to do at this end of the school year. Hayate knows so few people capable of such devotion.

Hayate decides that they must eat something before returning to work. They will be quick. Afafe will have more energy to study and her brother is very hungry. Hayate knows that Afafe loves pizza. She quickly convinces them.

They sit at a table at the pizzeria between Carthage and Tunis and ask to be served quickly. Afafe is very lively. The scene at the police station, with the ridiculous questions and comments and the grotesque nature of the farce cheers them up and makes them laugh until they cry. Afafe makes fun of them by repeating to Hayate all the obscenities and coarseness of the policemen. Hayate does not find it that funny but laughs along with her two companions, happy to be done with a formality that was weighing upon her. She realises to what extent Afafe needs to caricature and demystify a society and laws that constantly hold them back and oppress them. The burlesque scene they have just gone through sums up all that Afafe detests; she will be able to use it to support her feelings of rebelliousness. She will use it to make a mockery of authority and power.

On returning to the villa, Hayate organises her work in order not to waste the little time she has left. She unpacks boxes, hangs up some clothes and arranges her books and files, then starts to write her presentation for Saturday. At the end of the afternoon there is a ring at the door. It is Aïda and her daughter. Surprised and happy to see them, Hayate urges them to come in and have something to drink.

'I was worried about you,' says Aïda. 'What an incredible story! How did you spend the day? How do you feel?'

In a few words, Hayate tells her of her trip to the police station with Afafe.

'You were not very encouraging yesterday when I asked your advice about the statement. I didn't know what to do. But this morning, while speaking with Afafe, I realised that I had no choice. I had to go. I would be a coward if I let this man go free to carry on, without teaching him a lesson.'

'You know, last night I was very tired. I wasn't thinking clearly. On the one hand, you were right to register a complaint, but on the other, as you witnessed yourself, the reactions of the police show that the situation could have been dangerous for you. At the time, I didn't think about it, but I felt uneasy when you spoke about the police. If you had not been accompanied by the Tunisian police from the embassy, they could easily have bothered you and made you submit to humiliating, petty things. I know women friends who have been abused and terrified in those circumstances. They were not believed. They were told that they had provoked the attack and they were made to jump through all kinds of hoops to punish them. Here, victims are punished.'

Suddenly Hayate realises that she had forgotten Aïda's arrest, imprisonment and torture by the police at the time when she was demonstrating for a left-wing political party and denounced social injustice in her articles. It is not surprising that she should express this reaction with regard to the police. Hayate understands now her silence of the day before.

'It's not only here that victims are accused and punished! Everywhere in the world women who accuse their attackers are rarely taken seriously. Accusations are turned against them. People prefer not to believe them – society would have to change radically and it is not ready to do so. Often, these women are condemned and punished. I was afraid to register a complaint as well. When Afafe told me that she was ready to go with me, I realised that I had nothing to stop me. I don't know if I did a good thing or a bad thing, or if it will come to anything, but I feel like a load has been taken from me. You will stay and eat here. First, I'll fix us a drink. That will do us good after all the commotion of the past few hours. A gin and tonic? And what about your daughter? I have some good fruit juices. And I'd like you to stay the night. You'll have so many beds and rooms to choose from.'

Hayate prepares dinner, opening some tins of American food she has found in a cupboard. There is ravioli in tomato sauce, corn, chilli. Saïda is entranced by the novelty of this food and the fruit juices. There are also the famous American ices – chocolate, vanilla, pecan. Hayate does not particularly enjoy this cuisine. She prefers fruit, fresh vegetables and Tunisian cheese. The Tunisian wine is excellent. But she is happy to share new things with her guests and friends.

Saïda loves the ice cream; she is in heaven. She decides to take a bath in one of the villa's luxurious bathtubs. Hayate runs it for her with a bubble bath that makes light bubbles, full of multi-coloured reflections.

She pours a gin and tonic for Aïda and herself.

'I have my class tomorrow. I have to get up early to drive my daughter to school. I'm happy that I came – seeing you relax makes me feel better. The day has been exhausting and I'm afraid that Saturday's meeting will be stormy.'

'The conference? I've just started work on my presentation. It will mean days and nights of work. So much the better! It will help me to forget these last few days.'

'You must come to my place, too.'

'Of course! After the Club if you like. Have you seen Ahlame and Rima?'

'Ahlame is getting ready to leave for France. She really has decided to leave the country. I think she is creating illusions for herself, but there's nothing I can do to stop her. She has to go through it herself. Rima is exhausted like everyone else at the end of the school year. She has been attacked and criticised for her article, but she's in good spirits and carries on working. I admire her for not giving up.'

'I do too. Why are there so few people capable of such an ideal, such values? Will we be able to recruit others before it's too late?'

> I think of you Rima
> you who laugh without malice
> you who love without calculating
> you who tell of love flowered with swallows
> I see you writing a fertile peaceful land
> I think of you who have the power to be born
>   without limits
> without bitterness and without rivalries
> You have freed her hand
> You have given a voice to her pain
> Through words anguished and innovative

135

you have described the woman who dared
the march reconciling the irreparable
a dove with wings covering the bloodied city
In the silence, Ahlame speaks of departure
She refuses the women who curse her
those who bless her
all of these illusions holding back her creative power
She goes forth wounded by words
suffering, torn by the need to choose
She leaves with the bird of nights
She knows not that a hurdle awaits her
barricade, cruel wall
at the end of the road
There are words that wound
and from which one does not recover
Some raise a storm
Others, flat, that ricochet
off the smooth lagoon of lost memory
And there are those that kill

15

The garden smells of rose and jasmine and the sun is bursting with spring. A sea breeze is blowing. Hayate opens her windows wide and breathes in deeply this air of renewal that fills her with energy. For three nights she has worked until morning to finish her presentation for the meeting. She has plunged into work to forget her recent worries and the move that depressed her. She misses the view of the sea. Here, she is enclosed in a pretty square villa which is spacious and comfortable but barricaded for security reasons. She does not feel free to work in the garden. It is narrow and there are curious neighbours who watch her. She stays inside, climbing up to the terrace from time to time for a view of the hills, the villas in the pines, the white, green and brown against the deep blue sky which make up the landscape of El-Menzeh.

She has only her conclusion left to write. It is Friday, she must go to the city for a few hours to see Samia. She will finish her work in the evening and will have enough time before the meeting at the Club the following afternoon. While drinking her coffee, she jots down a few impressions in her diary:

Fatima, the landlord's wife, has asked me to take back my complaint. She was crying, saying that she was not sleeping any more, that her daughter who is about to give birth, was doing very poorly, that she was ready to serve me for free if I return to the house, and she'd give back my deposit. I told her that I did not understand her, that if I had gone to the police, it was also for her sake. How could she stand to be treated this way? Had she thought about the horror of her husband's actions, about justice, about other women to whom he had perhaps done the same thing, or even worse? She replied that he had always been very nice to her and their children. And she continued to beg me, holding my hands, kissing them, swearing to me that she would do everything in her

137

power to make life easy for me. Her big black eyes filled with tears had a strong effect. Her request troubled me. What did she want? Why was she not supporting what I had done? What did these words mean – that she would serve me, make my life easier? Already the slave of this man, was she asking me to use her as a slave, too? Did her concept of love signify servitude? Was it love that filled her with such chagrin, or the fear of dishonour, of the loss of a breadwinner, of punishment, of what others would say?

I still saw before me the face of this imploring woman. I was not sleeping well. I questioned my judgement. Had I done the right thing to lodge a complaint? Most of the women had not approved. Was I right to believe that I was serving the cause of women? Can an isolated gesture have a collective effect? Was the support of the embassy in this a help or a hindrance? Wouldn't it be seen as 'imperialist intervention'? One of the men I know told me: you are Lebanese but you react like an American woman. But he is not for the emancipation of women. One has only to see how he treats his wife. His remark resembles the argument – heard so often – that feminism is a western phenomenon that has no place in the Arab world. It is used by those who seek to weaken and divide the movement, the solidarity among women. Why attach importance to such words? Because I am troubled, I am not sure if I have done a good thing. Another woman told me that I should have arranged things amicably, asked some friends to go and speak to the landlord and demand that he excuse himself and promise that he will never do that again. According to her, that would have been a lot more effective. Another told me that I should have claimed some financial compensation. Then they would have taken me seriously. And how would I have managed if the embassy had not loaned me a house, if I had been forced to go to a hotel?

They can talk! writes Hayate in her diary. What would they have done in my place, if they had been frightened as I was, disoriented by panic? If the face of this woman, Fatima, was not haunting me, I would be sure that I'd done the best thing.

Several days later, the woman's face swollen with tears disappeared. It was replaced by that of a shrew. Hayate learned that the owner had already been under surveillance and was known for his depravity, that he owned clubs with a bad reputation and was suspected of having brothels in Paris, and that his wife supported him in all of this! I avoided her wisely, writes Hayate. This woman was holding out a carrot. In my usual sympathy for those who are suffering, I almost believed her! What a relief – I was right to complain!

Hayate puts some things in her bag and leaves to catch the bus. It does not come. Left to wait under a scorching sky as noon approaches, she calls a taxi, climbs in and gives the address of the research centre. In a few minutes they arrive. The building is situated at the entrance to the Médina. She is anxious about the confrontation awaiting her. As with the police, she knows that the process is necessary – painful but essential.

She knocks on Samia's office door and goes in. She is greeted coldly. She sits down and takes her courage in both hands.

'I came to see you,' she explains, 'because I don't like misunderstandings. I found out that you think I am seeing the friend with the guitar you invited to Rima's party. I am here to tell you that's not true. I can assure you that I am not interested in him and have never gone out with him. You told me that you no longer saw him after the party. If you had told me that you were continuing to see him, he would have interested me even less. The lovers of my friends are off limits.'

'I don't believe you. My best friend saw you with him. I trust her, not you.'

Samia appears stubborn and impenetrable.

'Really, Samia,' Hayate pleads. 'I was convinced that I was your friend, too. How can you believe that I would betray your trust in me? And how can you continue to believe this lie while I'm here telling you that it is absolutely untrue?'

Samia taps her pencil on the table. The expression on her face is bored and uncommunicative. In any case, she wants to cut short the discussion.

'Halima or Ahlame, or both of them, should not have told you what I told them. It's their fault.'

Hayate wonders how she knew that it was Ahlame and Halima who had spoken to her about this. She is more Machiavellian than she had thought. Why had she imagined this scenario when she no longer had any relationship with this man? And why had she chosen Hayate to accuse? It is clear that she is hiding something. But what? Hayate is full of bitterness and sadness. One last time she tries to reconcile the situation.

'You really don't want to believe me? I was hoping that we could renew our friendship. I realise you don't want to and that hurts.'

Samia does not react. Hayate continues, suddenly gripped with anger.

'If you had considered me a friend, you would have come to me directly when you had doubts, and you would have asked me to tell you what was happening. Since you preferred to listen to rumours, that must mean that it was convenient for you. You don't want to trust me because you need someone on whom to project your fantasies. This reinforces your behaviour and your view of life. Where is the solidarity of women in all of this? Have you dropped it from your concept of the feminist movement?'

Hayate is surprised by her own courage, shocked to have said some of what she felt. Usually, she does not respond so easily; she has a tendency to remain passive when someone attacks and tries to humiliate her. Where did all of this confidence come from?

During the entire tirade, Samia has not moved. She motions for Hayate to leave. Hayate goes, upset but also relieved to have expressed her disappointment. She takes big strides through the city streets. She forgets the stifling heat. In a few minutes she is perspiring profusely. She sees the International Café and goes in and orders an orange juice. Rima is there with some journalist friends. She waves for Hayate to join them. Hayate does not feel like talking with those outside her circle of close friends; she would prefer to see Rima alone. But she does not want to hurt her and there is no other table free. She approaches the group. Rima exclaims:

'You look so hot! Is everything all right?'

Hayate nods. The discussion is animated.

'We're organising a demonstration against the Syrian embassy,' Rima explains. 'What Syrian powers are doing now in Lebanon, exterminating Palestinians and supporting certain Shiite groups who are killing them, is intolerable. No one is reacting in the Arab world, or elsewhere. We have to express our disapproval.'

When her journalist friends have left, Rima asks her what is wrong. Hayate briefly explains her confrontation with Samia. Rima gives her opinion:

'Samia is going through a difficult time right now. I haven't been able to communicate with her for a while.'

'Has it been since the party?' asks Hayate.

'Yes! It's surprising, but it's true. I hadn't thought about it. Why the connection?'

'The attitude of a certain number of women towards me has changed since the party. I'm trying to understand what could have happened.'

'They had such a good time they feel guilty about it. We are not used to letting ourselves go in this way. I can tell you Hayate, I have never had such a good birthday, and I will not have another that good for a long time. Thank you for having offered the house. It was marvellous. Forget the others; they envy you, that's all.'

'I'm trying not to think about it any more, but it's difficult. Samia was a friend.'

'I told you, Samia is not doing well. She needs an outlet for her resentment. You're a foreigner. It's easier to sling mud at you than someone else. Haven't you noticed how xenophobic we Tunisians are?'

'Not more than other races. It's true that last year in Lebanon, despite the war in West Beirut, I was not criticised like I have been here because of my American grant. Actually, with everything that is happening there now, it would not have been hard to imagine. It's also true that I'm no stranger to Lebanese society.'

'Don't worry about it any more. Go and rest now and forget about it. It's not worth it. I have to go; I have so many things still to do, and this demonstration to organise.'

141

'When will it be?'

'Monday morning.'

'I don't know if I'll join you for the demonstration. As you know, I tried to organise a pacifist demonstration *for* peace and *against* no one. I feel no sympathy for the Syrian regime, far from it! I agree with your denunciation. But currently in Lebanon the only solution I see to unite people and have an effect is pacifistic acts of resistance.'

'I know what you mean. In any case, I was going to advise you not to join us. As a foreigner, it could be dangerous. You must look out for yourself.'

'See you tomorrow, at the meeting.'

'Yes, see you tomorrow.'

Coming out of the International Café, Hayate bumps into Nayla accompanied by some friends. She has not seen her since the death of her mother.

'We have finally organised the peace march, Hay,' Nayla tells her. 'We're meeting Monday in front of the Syrian embassy. You must be quite pleased.'

'No, Nayla, I'm not too happy about it. This is not the march for peace I had envisaged. This organised demonstration is like dozens of others that have failed. I wanted to organise a march *for* peace and not a demonstration *against* a regime, as corrupt as it may be. I understand your denunciation, but I don't think that it will have a real impact or that it will lead to a solution for Lebanon, for all those who suffer there, whatever side they are on. You may think that marches for peace are not any more successful. Symbolically, they have stood for something. They have united people, calmed them. They have filled so many civilians who couldn't take it any more with love and hope. Maybe they even gave those fighting something to think about. In any case, they have let us believe that the country can be reborn from its ashes. In Lebanon's current chaotic state, a success, even a symbolic one, has got to be a step forward. Shouldn't we dream, invent utopias to counter despair rather than perpetuate the same reactions, the same conflicts that the world has always known?'

'So you're letting us down? You won't be among us on Monday?'

'I've been advised against it. Remember, I'm a foreigner in this country. No one knows how the demonstration will end. Some of my close friends tell me that I would be better off keeping my distance. I am going to take their advice. I would have so liked to take part in a peace march! I would have been ready to face anything for that cause!'

'Too bad!' Nayla throws up her hands as if to say that the conversation has ended.

Hayate continues her walk, with her heart even heavier than after her confrontation with Samia. Nayla has never before appeared so cold and distant! Not a word about what has just happened to her. However she was the one who had helped her find the house in Salammbô and Hayate knows that everyone is aware by now of her unfortunate encounter with the landlord. Maybe she was reserved because she was not alone. As she is a discreet person, perhaps she is incapable of expressing her feelings, her sympathy, when others are there. Hayate looks for excuses to explain Nayla's behaviour. She does not want to admit that Nayla too has changed her opinion and is now on the side of those criticising her.

Hayate gets into a taxi. She is more depressed than she has been at any time since her arrival in Tunisia. She is almost happy that her stay is coming to an end. Apart from a few close friends who support her, she feels abandoned and alone. She has not done all the work she would have liked to do – too many frustrations, obstacles, conflicts. Nayla's attitude and words have completely demoralised her. How could Nayla have confused a peace march with the demonstration she is organising? Why did she change, close herself off? In the beginning, they had established good communication. Why did she decide to censure her own creation, her strikingly beautiful writing, so quickly destroyed? This change goes back to the party as well. That evening Nayla had become ill. She had gone to one of the bedrooms upstairs. Several days before, she had been so happy about this birthday celebration; she looked

143

forward to forgetting her worries and finally having some fun. Her illness was the result of this opening up; expressing herself in this way had made her feel guilty, sick. Once again Hayate wonders if the death of Nayla's mother will eventually allow her to express what she is holding inside; it is smothering her. She would love to see her unrepressed!

Hayate realises that these recent events have shown her that she has made some true friends. The confrontation with Samia showed her the courage of Halima and Ahlame. Samia's inevitable anger did not stop them from warning Hayate what people were saying behind her back. For them, truth, justice and solidarity among women are essential. They are ready to thwart the schemes, uncover the tricks, confront rival elements and their power games. Why not look at the positive side of the coin?

She arrives at El-Menzeh, pays the driver and goes into the villa as the phone is ringing – it's Paris.

'Hello, chérie. I've finally reached you. I was worried.'

'How did you get my number?'

'Not having heard from you, and unable to reach you at the other number, I contacted the embassy. They told me you had moved.'

'Yes, and you know, you were right to worry. The owner of the house I was renting attacked me . . .'

'He attacked you?' There was much concern in his voice.

'Did he hurt you?'

'He caused me a lot of fear and mental anguish. I had to go to the police to register a complaint.'

'And with the women? Is everything all right? I feel you are isolated.'

'What intuition! How did you know?'

'I felt it in your letters.'

'It's not like it was in the beginning. I'm trying to understand what has happened. I'll tell you all about it soon. And you? What are you doing now?'

'I'm preparing an issue on Iraq. It's difficult to find people ready and able to talk about the area. When do you return?'

'I'll be in Paris in about ten days.'

'I'll be expecting you.'

The line goes dead. The conversation, though brief, has comforted Hayate. This real friend understands her. He works in and loves, knows and grasps the complexities of this area of the world. His words came at the right time, just at the moment when Hayate needed to hear the voice of a friend to support her. She is happy about her return to Paris when they will be able to discuss all of this at great length, try to understand it and put a finger on the wound.

> In the pain of words
> On the path of the journey
> quarrels break out
> recriminations deepen
> resentment wells up
> small wars explode
> here and there
> a missile of blood crosses
> the monotonous meanness
> of a world which bends under the weight of hatred
> swollen with the venom of vengeance
> the Earth cracks open at every fissure
> she does not straighten herself
> Men continue to possess her
> without heeding her cry of alarm
> Pushed to more insanity
> to more precise and murderous attacks
> a repetition of rape that nothing stops
> the men labour her emaciated flanks
> she teeters under their anger
> falls into madness
> And yet in the night of forgetting
> red flowers have sprung forth
> buds of apple flowers have burst open
> spreading their sweet calming perfume

friendly hands have broken chains
the chains that held the dispossessed
an elixir of love has filled famished stomachs
eyes have been opened to the harvests of peace
wine crop bandaging the wounds
stopping the gale of hatred
collecting foam from the crest of words
mixing the honey of sunny mornings
adorning the houses of return
Orient of my suffering
Oh, the transparency of words!

16

Aïda gives birth to the running water of burned
	forests,
the blue source streaming under the silent branches
her arms open to life's call
hands stretching out to others
forming a chain of tenderness
She avoids quarrels, insults
meanness
She seeks harmony
the beauty of a moonlit night
a rewooded land, replanted gardens
Rima moves toward the fountain of reconciliation
pulling in from all the corners of the Earth
clans pacified by its cooling waters
She gives meaning to the unnameable
She finds words for the unthinkable
Ahlame traces a brilliant star in the ravine
sign of love, gratitude, fusion
There is so much suffering within her
each of her words is a wound
Halima builds multiple bridges
over the tumultuous waters of vengeance
Like a delicate swallow
she collides with the archways of night
Afafe transmits a passion without boundaries
uniting the dispossessed, the excluded
She has filled her pockets with dreams and with
	vision
Sihame weaves houses without doors

welcoming the martyrs, the suffering
She works for justice
until exhaustion sets in
Lilia plants the seed of imagination
in each expectation
in each desire
Nayla seeks the kernel of existence
a vision of the Milky Way
she cannot attain
Samia loses herself in purulent phobias
a neurosis engendered by fear
Fatima fabricates bitterness from innocents
perfidious ruse of the depraved
Jelila unravels the parchment of knowledge
inscribing there signs of a feminism, a humanism
Zanède announces the opening of a space
where the body would unfurl its freedom
Malika paints the migrating bird
uniting all the disinherited
Hala cuts the cord of those hung
delivers them from asphyxiation
Nebiha draws a swallow for lost childhood
a path of return for the dispossessed
Khedija too, full of vigour
full of luminous presence
dies in the early morning
Hédia brings to the song the wings of a poem
She has traced all with a single stroke
so that nothing will be erased
And me, I try to give to each of these meetings
to each of these privileged moments
to each of these readings
to each exchange
to each dialogue
to each sorrow
to each gesture

to each misunderstanding
to each wound,
to each word
to each lyric
its hidden meaning
I seek within the pain of words
a balm for my suffering
an elixir for the ills of these women
I spell each name
each memory
so that nothing will be lost
so that one day the children of these friends
will understand the courage of their mothers
and take up the torch
So that other women
elsewhere
in other times
in other places
will be comforted
will no longer feel alone

Hayate is at the Club Taher Haddad where a meeting is being held on the topic 'Which feminism for the Maghreb?' She notes: 'Why don't they say "which" in the feminine? Language – French in particular – has so many barriers; how does one scale the problems attached to it? It is necessary to create another language, another mode of expression, through song, poetry and the creation of new words which correspond better to new ideas, which will break the syntax, the hierarchy, the traditional dualism which perpetuates oppression and restrains liberty. I have learned so many things here this year. This Tunisian experience has been enlightening. The new journal, the Club, the women, are a reflection of the society. People must speak out and formulate fundamental questions in order to find solutions for their problems. But is this for me to do? Here I have lived all the tragedies of the Arab world, and I have seen Lebanon from afar, through the perspective of

149

another Arab country. I have witnessed unselfishness, great indifference, and deceptive propaganda. Except for a few women who express through their life and their new journal some real problems – saving the Earth, participating by means of active resistance, helping youth and women, finding creative means of expression, by incorporating all of that into a different concept of the relationships between the sexes – I have been disappointed and have suffered as a result. I plunged myself with passion and interest into this group, identifying with these women. I have lived with them and their problems. Maybe I should talk about it one day, write it down, add my personal experience, write about what I have witnessed.'

This afternoon the atmosphere at the Club is heavy and agitated. The papers delivered are stamped with aggression; with all the noise, the opinions of others are not respected. The reactions are violent and often mean. Hayate wonders how she is going to read her paper, already a contested topic. She is full of apprehension. She listens as if in a fog to the problems mentioned – identity, relationship to language and to culture, the threat of fundamentalism, the lack of civil rights for women, what it means to be Arab, Tunisian, of the Maghreb, and their relationship to feminism.

She grasps passages from presentations and personal accounts; she is stirred by what strikes her as original or touching. Hala asks what feminism is with regard to political activism; are they tightly linked or is the liberation of women a global social project demanding legislative, political, economic and educational reforms? In a situation dominated by cultural, political and socio-economic identity crises, where do their priorities lie? Can the oppression of women disappear through the sole effort of feminist women?

Hala distinguishes three kinds of feminist movements: the reformist – trying to make conditions better for women; the radical – not satisfied by simple reforms, challenging the foundations of the patriarchal society; and the ideological – mixing the class struggle with the gender struggle. She is convinced that the women of Tunisia must combine the three approaches and take militant action: a feminist struggle allowing them to acquire full democratic citizenship and following up with socio-economic structural changes. The dominant patriarchal ideology slows up the contribution of Tunisian women. The misogynist attitudes and especially the Islamic movements are a real danger to the rights, liberty and equality of women. She observes that feminist movements in Tunisia contain elements necessary for a transformation of the entire society, for their struggle combines the fight against exploitation, imperialism, and against the specific oppression of women.

An animated discussion follows Hala's presentation. Then it is Aïda's turn; she is troubled by the aggressive atmosphere of the meeting and stumbles over her words. She looks for her papers, excusing her lack of organisation and her presentation in the form of a personal account. She says that she hesitated, not knowing whether her experience would be interesting. In her faltering introduction, there is a kind of plea for more tolerance and more love, but the audience is rigid and gives no sign of encouragement.

Aïda speaks for a long time; the longer she speaks, the more confidence she gains. She pours out her heart, talks about her marriage, her abortions and her imprisonment. In the middle of a sentence, a word, she wipes away her tears. She stops, then carries on. Hayate would like to console her, but doesn't dare.

Aïda explains that she has come to feminism through an emotion. For her, feminism is essentially a new relationship among women, based on trust, solidarity and love. This is why she becomes depressed when she senses aggression, intolerance and egotism in the creation of their journal, in their meetings and in her relationship with the other women. She is idealistic and intends to stay that way. The war of 1967, of Israel against the Arabs, made her conscious of her Arab identity. She felt vulnerable in the face of the other, the West. She cannot bear intolerance and elitism. Thanks to the Club, she has had the strength to affirm her marginality and her political view.

When she was arrested in 1974, she had already realised that one could not start a revolution by reproducing old systems of

151

power: hierarchy, discipline, the absence of democratic debate, paternalistic relationships with others. Despite a painful experience, she has a marvellous memory of intense relationships of love and solidarity that existed among militants – women and men – facing repression. Revolution is the transformation of society through democratic practice in trade-union and professional institutions, or in informal frameworks. In a country where there is no freedom of expression, no community life, and where the individual is isolated, the Club has brought her hope for change. Democratic freedom is inseparable from solidarity with the oppressed.

At the end of her presentation, Hayate approaches her; she tells her briefly how much she appreciated her direct and personal style of speaking. It had taken much courage. She squeezes her hand. Aïda is nervous. Her speech has exhausted her; the unfriendly atmosphere in the room has not made her feel relaxed. She asks Hayate for a cigarette and lights it while another takes the floor. She was expecting reactions or questions but her appeal receives no response at all from this audience seemingly untouched by emotions expressed in such a direct way. Other presentations follow.

Ahlame's turn. Calm and poised, she articulates each word, each sentence very slowly, with clarity. She reads one of her stories on the loss of virginity with a great deal of expression and strength, pain and sweetness, using flowery and provocative language. She breaks the silence surrounding her own womanhood in order to end oppressive self-censorship. She states that the silence of feminists concerns the specificity of a woman's body, relationships between women, and politics. There is silence about the menstrual period, virginity, masturbation, pleasure in general, abortion, childbirth, etc. The list is long!

Why does she suffer, seeing veiled women lightly signing over the death of their body? This also represents a growing threat to the gains so heavily paid for by Tunisian women. Why does she cry when her neighbour is beaten up? Why does she feel personally humiliated? Because the experience of these women reflects a larger picture of her own condition, in which obtaining respect from others is a perpetual struggle. Their servitude sets limits on her own growth.

Ahlame introduces the problem of women's jealousy of each other, mainly spread through gossip. Feminism and gossip, there is a contradiction in terms. She recalls being the subject of rumours the day after her presentation 'Feminism and fecundity', delivered at the previous year's conference. It was then she learned that she was thought to be a prostitute (that gave her some ideas), that she was divorced (her husband was happy to hear the news), that she was a lesbian, a husband stealer (unfortunately the number of men was not mentioned), that she was scandalous because she refused to become a mother. Gossip, explains Ahlame, aims to destroy what is disturbing. It tends to lend a sense of security to the person (man or woman) who spreads it. It shows the anguish caused by setting oneself apart from others and seeks to disarm the feeling of guilt. The accusations of prostitution and husband-stealing are the projection of personal fantasies. They signify the desire for a freer experience of the body, of a better assumed sexuality. Homosexuality is of the same order. To dare to say this taboo word in a presentation could only mean that one has tried it. The scandalous refusal to have children indicates above all the resistance of women, their unconscious refusal to push back the limits, to question the idea that sexuality can do without the sacrosanct finality of procreation.

According to Ahlame, rumours and hostility demoralise the women for whom solidarity among women is sacred, but these same women would not go so far as to defend homosexuality, or even articulate it, for it involves them too heavily in subversion. This is a point of no return because society does not pardon the choice of this path that seems to question the fundamental elements of society; it is not procreative and affirms the right to have pleasure – ideas which are linked to anarchy. The Third World is characterised by a feeling of duty, of repressive laws. However, the contradiction is flagrant, for society favours homosexuality by cultivating hatred between the sexes, social inequality, ignorance, and therefore fear of the other, by banishing mixed groups.

Ahlame uses a principle formulated by a number of psychiatrists – that every being is bisexual at its origin. Society then takes it upon itself to sexually mutilate the part judged to be out of keeping with the attributes of one's gender. She talks about excision for girls and circumcision for boys. The girl grows up in an ambivalent emotional climate: love and hate for the mother. Does the autonomy of feminists take root in the profound desire to reinstate the mother-daughter relationship? The absence of a physical reference adds to the emotional ambivalence of the mother. The little girl has no penis like the father; no breasts or pubic hair like the mother. There is still a point of commonality in the clitoris, but no one wants to talk about it ... Behind the husband is the mother's shadowy profile. Is it not he who takes responsibility for the wife, gives her affection, awakens the body and enhances its value? It is everything that her mother could not do. It is he who brings to life this woman who has not yet really seen the light of day. But he is also in search of a mother. The law of the strongest wins out; the woman finds herself in the situation of giving what she does not really have: love. The emotional hole within her deepens. The husband changes into a bad mother through the intervention of the mother-in-law. Afterwards, the woman turned mother herself is still a child inside and the circle begins again.

Ahlame emphasises one final point – that of jealousy in love relationships. The woman who incites our jealousy is the one we imagine taking our place, stealing our deepest being, our body. Jealousy is even greater when there is internal repression and great dissatisfaction. It's as if love and pleasure are threatened once shared. It's as if what one gives to the other has been taken from us. The jealousy is just as great as the love, the admiration. The object of our jealousy could have been a model, a comforting support, and thus a replacement for the mother. Instead, it is transformed into anguish, from which comes an intense feeling of deception, of loss. Jealousy is also the expression of a lack of confidence in one's self which reappears with each identification problem. It is easy to understand why intellectuals have spoken so little about this human relationship, because analysis and rationalisation do not protect one from jealousy.

Someone in the room accuses Ahlame of being dogmatic. She replies, without faltering, that she must be allowed to be dogmatic once in her life if she wants. No question of real importance is raised. Either the subject does not inspire interest, or the way she talks is disturbing, or both. Ahlame retires to a corner of the room with a faraway look and an ironic smile on her lips as she listens to the other speakers. Hayate would like to go up to her and tell her how much she appreciated the originality and clarity of her analysis, the importance of what she expressed so well, but the atmosphere in the room is so heavy that she remains glued to her chair, paralysed.

Samia and Malika present 'Social Images of Feminism in Tunisia'. Their research was prompted by the upsetting feeling provoked by the other's gaze – be it man or woman – an outsider to feminist knowledge and action. To this malaise was added a quest for recognition, and therefore a search for identity. The questions raised and elaborated on during meetings revolve around the definition of the movement seen from within and without, their capacity for action, the link between the condition and oppression of women and other societal problems, and the new contribution of feminism to these liberation struggles.

Samia and Malika show the discourse between the women's movement and the fundamentalist movement. They explain how the fundamentalist movement, wanting to oppose the government, has criticised the personal status code, questioned its existence, called for revision and a return to Islamic legislation. The feminists and progressive movements saw fundamentalism as a threat not only to the rights of women but also to the process of democracy new to this country. People questioned spontaneously called to mind feminism and fundamentalism, for both are confronting the same problem of Tunisian identity. Concerning women, fundamentalists and feminists have diametrically opposed views. But

155

each supports social projects. Feminists take an individualistic viewpoint alien to traditional Tunisian society; fundamentalists question the rights of Tunisian women, in particular the right to work outside the home, which has led to irreversible societal changes.

Samia and Malika end with a series of recommendations and suggestions to reorient the thinking and debate on the reality of the Tunisian Arab-Muslim woman, while producing texts addressing the history of women's movements in Tunisia. They suggest doing research on areas which allow emancipation within the culture in order to avoid the accusation of conforming to western ideas. They want to see an association created, to establish a plan of action and work hard to bring it to completion by raising the consciousness of as many rural and illiterate women as possible, making them aware of the rights they have and those they have yet to acquire. They want to fight against the rise of fundamentalism by writing newspaper articles, while bringing to light contradictions within this movement. They want to invest in the cultural camp, by presenting other models and changing the way children are educated. Finally, in their writing, they want to avoid shocking the sensitive Arab-Muslim society, which would only increase aggression.

Hayate wonders why Samia cannot make the connection between what she says and her actions. To suggest avoiding an aggressive tone and then to insult others – the contradiction is evident. Why does she not act with tact and sensitivity in her relationships with the women of this group first and foremost? She notes also that her conclusion shows a fear of being seen as too westernized, or not Arab enough, rather than affirming her identity. What Samia and Malika are saying is that they are westernized, but they do not wish to show it. Everyone has been influenced by the West. In their insistence on not wanting to be identified with the West, there is a counter-racism at work. For Hayate, racism that purports to be anti-racist is still racism. She understands the desire of the oppressed to affirm their identity but, like Sartre in *Black Orpheus*, she thinks this can only be a stage, a necessary step one must go beyond in order to arrive at true humanism. Hayate is convinced that one must go further, and not remain fixed in paralysing claims of exclusion. With humanism, one must have the contribution of women; this half of humanity must be included in a process of true liberation.

A listener, an American woman and Middle Eastern scholar known for her work on Iran, asks for the floor. Without great enthusiasm, the audience allows it. She stands up, and speaking French with a strong American accent, she says that these debates remind her of those in Iran before its revolution. She explains the research she is doing on women in Tunisia and in the world today, the Middle East in particular. She has contacted fundamentalist women in Tunisia and has observed and questioned them. They were open and frank with her. She noted that these fundamentalists were much more organised than other groups of women and that they have tangible solutions to real problems in society. They are leading benevolent work which supports their communities and they are close to the people, to women and their concerns. She is convinced that herein lies the real danger for women of the Middle East, and that if nothing is done to overcome this movement, it will be catastrophic, resulting in a political takeover as seen in Iran.

She sits down. The room does not react. Hayate is at first stunned by their silence. Then she realises that the silence indicates disdain for the nationality of the one who has spoken, and scorn for what she has said. The atmosphere is icy. Hayate is troubled by what she has just heard. What lack of tact and understanding concerning Tunisia and the women's movement! How could she confuse causes and effects? The danger stems not from fundamentalism but from poverty. It is not surprising that a country like the United States which consumes two thirds of global production is detested, especially when it preaches the dangers of fundamentalism! How can this scholar criticise the women of the Club she hardly knows and whose progress and work she has not studied?

Hayate realises that she is herself a victim of the arrogant

157

conduct of certain American intellectuals. This arrogance appals the women of the Club, and increases their aggressive stance toward the U.S. As the beneficiary of an American grant, Hayate pays for the lack of sensitivity and understanding of the person who has just spoken. On the other hand, she realises that some women who do not know her put them together, but those she has met should know how to distinguish between their views. She wonders how to make her presentation in such an atmosphere. Still, she must show that there are other voices, other movements in the United States, struggles that are on the side of the oppressed and women who suffer. To make herself the advocate of the U.S – or any other country – disturbs her, but she has no choice. She has already committed herself and must go through with it, despite the distress, the tightening in her throat.

She shows that American feminism has taken up at least three currents of contemporary thought: the notion of the rights of man, of the citizen, a socialist theory, that affirms the right to economic and political justice, and the analysis of sexual behaviour within a social and political context. Feminism stems from these three currents – political, economic and sexual – and at the same time transforms them, because for the first time, women seek to obtain rights in all of these spheres. Feminism is revolutionary because it adheres to a goal of world-wide social justice. Feminism is a universal idea, but does not deny differences in women's experiences, according to race, class, nationality or religion. Dialogue between these differences is crucial for the development of a truly international feminist movement.

There are founding principles for different feminist currents. Radical feminism poses sexual oppression as the oldest, deepest form of exploitation; it precedes that of race and class. Socialist feminism holds that sexual oppression is contained in class oppression and stems from capitalism; capitalism must therefore be eliminated for women to obtain freedom. For bourgeois feminism, the liberation of women can be realised without profound economic and political changes within the structures of contemporary capitalist democracies. Cultural feminism is not so interested in

158

the political and economic agenda, but rather concentrates on the development of an independent feminine culture.

Hayate then summarises the different authors and works of American feminists of the '70s, a rich era for American feminism. In 1970, Kate Millet published her book, *Sexual Politics*, which has become a feminist classic. In it she shows how the subordination of women is historical and dialectic. She questions Freud in particular and makes the distinction between sex and its biological attributes and gender and its cultural and social attributes. She refers to the work of Margaret Mead and to her anthropological research of the '20s and '30s in which she demonstrated that in certain cultures attributes considered here to be feminine and masculine are reversed.

In *Masculine World, Feminine Place*, Elizabeth Janeway shows how a 'social mythology' reinforces patriarchy. Like Millet, she accuses sociologists and psychologists of describing women not as they are, but rather as they think they should be. Janeway affirms that many women accept this 'mythology' because they get something from it. They agree to exchange private power for public submission.

Shulamith Firestone, in *Dialectic of Sexuality*, suggests a deepening of historical materialism, which she thinks extends beyond Marx and Engels. It is in shedding the physical and psychological responsibility for the reproduction of the species that women will liberate themselves. Mitchell reproaches Firestone for not speaking about women's oppression in a specifically historical context because, she says, women live in two worlds – that of production and that of reproduction – and they are oppressed in both.

Michelle Rosaldo, in an essay titled 'Global Theoretical View', declares that inequality between the domestic and the public is common in all forms of social organisation. She shows that when men are implicated in domestic life, the distance between men and women and the degree of authority that men exercise over women diminishes.

Sherry Ornter, in her essay, 'Is the Feminine to the Masculine What Nature is to Culture?' says that culture is considered not

159

only as separate from nature, but superior to it, because it is able to control and transform the environment. Women associated with nature are devalued. In other words, 'because women give life, men create culture'. Women are considered closer to nature, as intermediaries between nature and culture, while men control culture.

In *Against Our Will: Men, Women and Rape*, Susan Brown-miller declares that rape is the secret weapon which reinforces patriarchy. The significance of rape is attached to the representation of women as property. Laws punishing rape in the Codes resemble laws regarding property damage. She cites the example of war where raping means conquering. Rape, historically invented by men, has been a means of controlling women through fear. Studies of rape show that the rapist is not an abnormal or abject individual, but rather ordinary, even commonplace.

Susan Griffin, in 'Rape: The American Crime Par Excellence', writes of the masculine fraud which tries to show women that they need masculine protection because they can be raped. The system fails to mention that the protector is often the rapist himself. Griffin links the crime of rape to American crimes against other countries, especially in the context of Vietnam. The experience of rape crosses distinctions of class and race.

Then Hayate explains how the statement 'the personal is political' has become a catch phrase for feminist movements, the theorists as well as activists. She talks of groups like 'Conscious Raising' which function somewhat like the Club Taher Haddad and have helped women to move forward individually as well as collectively. Thanks to these groups, women have realised that what they have to say is as important as what the authorities, the experts, the recognised holders of knowledge, have said about them. They discover that they as women are not alone, that their experience and feelings are symptomatic of a society. These groups create a bridge between the public and the private, enabling the private to express itself publicly and organise itself politically. The method used by the women to react to one another within the group is founded on a feminist principle that seeks to put theory into practice: to create a space while meeting regularly at a given moment, and to be equal, each woman having an equal right to speak, one experience having no more value than another. These groups are also therapeutic, for they encourage women to talk about the wounds caused by their experience.

About the middle of the 1970s, Gerda Lerner, Adrienne Rich, Susan Griffin and other feminists begin to discuss a feminist concept of analysis which places women 'in the centre', with the experience of women becoming the primary source for cultural values. An aspect of this theory of the 'woman in the centre' is the lesbian point of view. Lesbians declare that their preference is more than sexual, it is political. A woman who no longer needs masculine approval is no longer his hostage. If the personal is political, the choice of woman in a personal relationship has great political importance. Due to their sexual preference, lesbians are free to seek their emotional nourishment from other women rather than from men. Adrienne Rich criticises feminist theories for not treating heterosexuality as a political institution. She thinks that heterosexuality is instilled by all sorts of mechanisms tied to male power: physical violence, sexual slavery, rape, the ideology of romantic love.

In *Women and Madness*, Phyllis Chesler studies the disastrous results of the social conditioning of sexual roles. Women, to be feminine, are expected to be non-aggressive, dependent, to feel the need to be led, be affectionate, doubt themselves, be incapable of being robust and having an autonomous existence. These stereotypes lead women to failure, to victimisation and to insanity. A woman who refuses to conform to social and family norms – in other words, to be feminine – is compelled *not* to succeed. The 1970s see a reexamination of motherhood. Until then, feminism and motherhood had been seen as diametrically opposed, but towards the middle of the 70s, the question is reopened and frequently discussed.

In her book, *Of Woman Born*, Rich rejects the belief in a matriarchal period of history but talks of a 'gynocentrism,' as 'the organisation of certain societies'. Women see the world differently

161

from men, are not subject to the duality of western philosophy, to the division between spirit and body – one way for men to make women the object. If the institution of motherhood could be destroyed, women oppressed by the system of reproduction could be freed to accomplish other things.

The psychologist Dinnerstein shows how the experiences of early childhood form us. Because boys are completely controlled by women during infancy, they fear dependence on a single woman later in life. This is why they are polygamous and separate sexuality and love. Men's fear of women will continue as long as women keep a monopoly on the education of children. Men have to share this responsibility.

How is it that women continue to assume the responsibility of motherhood to the exclusion of men? asks Chodorow. It starts with the way women raise girls and boys differently. Sexual inequality will disappear if men as well as women participate in the maternal role. Masculine identity is conflicting because men have to reject identification with the mother of their childhood, while women do not. Men have to define themselves as non-women because they have been raised by women but cannot become women.

Keller brings up the question of the relationship between feminism and science. The scientific world is associated with masculinity, and culturally dominated by men. The point of view that science is the quintessential domain of objectivity, attracts a certain type of man, the one who rejects his feminine side. Scientific research and results are necessarily affected by this. Feminists must begin by criticising the basis of western scientific culture.

Hayate says that she will conclude by discussing the third phase of feminism in the 1970s. During this decade, the thesis of 'woman at the centre' was developed further. The difference between men and women which was deplored before this time (particularly by Simone de Beauvoir) becomes then a source of liberation.

In her book, *Gyn/Ecology*, Mary Daly plays with language as do the French feminists such as Cixous, Gauthier, Chawaf, Irigaray, Wittig, etc. They establish sexual difference through the manipulation of words, sentences, the language. 'Gynaecology,' the scientific study of women by men, becomes the science of women by women, the feminine knowledge of the feminine. Daly writes: 'All of the energy and power of men is extracted from women.' She calls this process 'necrophilia'.

In 1976, a group was formed in San Francisco: 'Women against the violence of pornography and the media'. The group launched a campaign against pornography by denouncing brutal photos in *Playboy* and *Hustler*. Robin Morgan declared that to accept pornography showing women tortured and destroyed is to accept a form of 'sexual fascism', and encourages rape, battery, and all sorts of violent acts toward women. 'Pornography is the theory,' she declared, 'rape is the practice.' For Griffin, pornography is the expression of hatred of the body, a central theme of western Christian morality; pornography destroys the erotic. On the other hand, Pat Califia accuses the women's movements against pornography as a return to Puritanism and traditional morality. 'Violence against women will not be reduced by increasing sexual repression,' she declares.

Many feminists, especially in the latter half of the 1960s, rejected Marxism and the left as hypocritical, fighting against oppression from one side only. They maintained that patriarchy, rape, lesbianism, pornography, etc. need more than a Marxist analysis. To acknowledge patriarchy and capitalism as the only sources for the oppression of women, is to ignore the complexity of sexuality. Thinkers such as Fanon, Marcuse and Laing have shown the importance of psychology in politics; feminists take up this idea, but do not always make the connection with economic and social structures. For them, feminist radicalism commits another error by wanting to universalise the female experience; they often ignore specifics like ethnicity, class and culture. Black and coloured women in particular accuse certain feminists of an unconscious racism. Angela Davis, notably, shows that the feminist analysis of rape fails to explain the historical reasons for the black rapist. Falsely universalising feminism thus would render it neo-colonialist and neo-imperialistic. It is a false universalism to say 'all women'. Hayate finishes with the discovery by American feminism of the pluralism of women's experience which evokes the specificity of feminism in Arab countries and in Tunisia.

A French woman declares that Hayate's presentation has nothing to do with Tunisian problems: rape, pornography, lesbianism are the prerogative of western countries, rich industralised countries that can afford the luxury of sexuality with all of the excesses that it brings; countries of the Third World are much too occupied with survival to think of these perversions. Hayate remarks that this attitude is pater/maternalistic, even racist. Why wouldn't people of the Third World be interested in sexuality? It is a desire which is just as urgent and important as others. What does she think of love and feelings attached to sexuality? Are they also a luxury for people of the Third World?

In an aggressive tone, Nayla wants to know where the relationship lies between the American feminism she has talked of and what is happening in Tunisia. Other women speak in a critical tone but without direct reference to what she has commented on. Hayate detests this type of polemic and does not respond. Ahlame, on the other hand, announces that she has learned a lot from Hayate's talk. For the first time, she has heard a clear presentation of the movements and ideas of American feminists. She is very grateful for this presentation and asks for a copy of it.

Sihame arrived late and out of breath towards the end of Hayate's paper. She apologises; she was working on an urgent project. She is small and slender with a round face and sparkling eyes. Her robust way of speaking and thinking belie her fragile appearance. She declares that she wants to take up the ideas of universalism, neo-imperialism and neo-racism outlined by Hayate, and analyse the relationship between feminism and cultural identity. At the beginning, she cites a left-wing Tunisian intellectual who declared that it is in French that Tunisians have learned to express themselves in order to have their say in the project for a human community. Arabic does not aptly express certain modes of thought, especially in the area of philosophy. This is particularly true for modern ideologies: socialism, marxism, etc. Trade unionism is also expressed in French.

Despite the new national awareness of people who are now liberated, this type of thinking remains, persists, and the cultural neo-colonialism of the Third World is perpetuated. The process by which cultures are rendered uniform and impoverished threatens even western nations that were once colonisers. The intelligent elite of developing countries entertains an inferiority and lack of power complex with regard to western models and cultural frameworks, while fighting for economic and political independence within each country.

Sihame would like the following questions addressed: does the establishment of feminism that demands a distinct social status for women mean the negation of cultural identity? Does the recovery of women's dignity necessarily have to place itself within the national culture?

Sihame says that she has looked for a definition of feminism and cultural identity. She has encountered difficulties regarding cultural identity. The existence of a group presupposes ethnocentrism, necessary for the affirmation of a group with regard to others. Every group affirms its superiority. To put oneself apart from others is to put oneself above them. This claim to an identity is manifested with even more vigour if the group is attacked by another trying to imitate it.

If we define feminism in a general way, as women reclaiming all rights, we see that it is a universal trend, but always diverse in content. It is not expressed in the same terms at any moment in time, or across all societies.

Universality thus contains a trap. It acts as a uniform agenda necessary for all societies, and not only as a trend towards a reclamation of dignity. It is therefore the continuation of neo-imperialism, since it affirms itself as a superior western model, tending to destroy and negate different agenda. It is burdened with a certain number of western models, having for its role a negation of the differences of other societies, the accomplishment of progress, modernity, superior values, in contrast to the backward condition of women in the societies it seeks to dominate.

Feminism in Tunisia was born out of a crisis of the model on which the former society was built and of the development of the family. Taher Haddad's approach was to say: We can find in our culture, our traditions, that with which to reaffirm the status of women, rather than turning towards the western model which uses our weakness in this domain to destroy the whole of society. Feminism was born at the same time as trade unionism, and has the same origin – the introduction of capitalism. For Sihame, the fact that feminism came from the West along with capitalism does not devalue feminism. It is the meanings that one attaches to it that can be negative.

The condition of women is the weak point of our societies and thanks to this the West attacks them. This aggression takes place through language. Arab accusations of the westernisation of feminism are confirmed by the choice of the language we use. We express ourselves in French and feminism becomes the negation of identity. Feminism, in this sense, gives reason to fundamentalism. We will have no hope of liberation unless we are capable of exposing the attack on our identity and pulling the rug out from under the feet of fundamentalists on this weak point.

Sihame finishes her presentation. She appears exhausted. Several times, she stopped to catch her breath and drink great gulps of water. Her paper raises many questions and reactions. Ahlame declares that she considers identity a false problem, and sees any discussion of identity as anti-feminist. Identity is duty while she demands desire. For Zaïnabe, identity should not be presented as a return to the source, but rather as an affirmation of one's place in the twentieth century, in the world. It is true that she was born into the framework of an Arab-Muslim culture, but she has established her own path and the perception of her own identity through her reading.

In a burst of emotion, Aïda takes the floor and begins by saying that she finds it very difficult that she does not express herself in Arabic. She has the feeling that a part of her has been destroyed.

She is frustrated that she is not able to communicate better with many people; writing in Arabic would allow her to reach them. What are we, who are we? she says, in a tear-filled voice, we who express ourselves in French? Halima, on the other hand, announces that she does not have a problem with language, for the day she decided to open her mind to learning, she discovered that language poses no limits, especially when one possesses the knowledge of several. Rather, it was enriching. It is only when language oppresses that it becomes a problem. She says that one should read writers who discuss this topic in many languages; there is so much to learn. Hayate notices that, unlike Aïda, Halima reads and writes Arabic fluently. This is perhaps the reason she is open to languages, at ease with them, while Aïda, belonging to a generation where French was imposed through colonisation, sees this lack as a wound inflicted by the dominant group.

> I write in the language of love
> I accompany it with the rhythm of the strings of the
>   lute
> of the guitar, of the drum
> My voice is a song crossing barriers
> a sweet sound of flute from Orient to Occident
> No border in the words gathered
> on the roads of countries which call to me
> I discover them in symbolic signs
> deciphered from pages open
> to my hope of understanding
> of communicating
> of finding meanings that sparkle in the sun
> or in the light of a candle
> I invent a melody for each name
> I trace a drawing for each wound
> I give a colour to each word
> thousands of rainbows circling the Earth

17

Aïda has organised a small farewell party at her house before Ahlame and Hayate leave Tunisia, and also in order to celebrate the end of the school year, the conference, the women's activities and the beginning of the summer holidays. Close friends are there: Hayate, Halima, her sister and daughter, Hadi, Aïda's Palestinian friend, who is shattered because the P.L.O. is sending him to Cyprus with other Palestinians, and there is also Rania, a neighbour and member of the Club Taher Haddad, with her husband and children. Ahlame will be arriving later with a friend. Rima and Sihame are bringing pastries.

In the kitchen, Hadi prepares hummus, baba-ghannouje and manaïches. Hayate is helping her. Halima washes the tomatoes, cucumbers and peppers for a Tunisian méchouïa. A happy Aïda hums a tune while straightening up the house. Her daughter Saïda and the other children run laughing from one room to the next.

Halima turns to Hayate.

'I'm sad you're leaving. We like having you here. We'll miss you so much.'

'I'm going to miss you too. I'll come back, or perhaps you'll visit me in a peaceful Lebanon!'

'Beirut!' exclaims Hadi. 'It's the most beautiful city in the world. I have a crazy nostalgia for Beirut. I'd like to go back there. Even in the midst of war and bombings, it is a fabulous city!'

'Fortunately, you didn't say that the destruction has made it a marvellous city! Many writers and novelists describe characters attracted by the violence and the ruins of Beirut; they think destruction is necessary to change society. They wish that this devastation would spread to other cities of the world. This is frightening and repugnant. That anyone can enjoy crime, pillage, demolition, suffering, despair, ruin – the death of a city and its inhabitants, is monstrous.'

As usual, and particularly when he's depressed, Hadi has drunk a little too much, and has not really understood Hayate's comments.

'You can't know,' he announces with pathos, in a tear-filled voice, 'but you have to understand to what extent I love Beirut. Beirut is magical. During the Israeli invasion, I was responsible for the wounded and dead. I drugged myself every day in order to carry out my job which consisted of going to look for them under the rubble after the bombings. This city which was burying our people was still very alive and had a surreal beauty. I miss it terribly. I have never felt in exile in Beirut. In Tunis, I feel uprooted. I wish I didn't have to go to Cyprus.'

'Why not go elsewhere?' asks Rania, entering the kitchen.

'Where else is there?' cries Hadi, despairingly.

'He has no choice,' says Aïda. 'The Palestinians have no passports or legal papers allowing them to live where they want. Do you understand? Imagine if you had no papers. It's as if someone has taken your identity. You can't do anything. You are the prisoner of the country which takes you in as a refugee.'

'That's the real identity problem,' takes up Halima, 'and not what we discussed at the meeting – language, fundamentalism, imperialism, culture. Hadi shows us a problem that is real and concrete.'

'But all of these problems are related,' maintains Aïda. 'We can't separate them. The splits and conflicts of the Arab world are linked to the condition of the Palestinian people.'

'And to the tragedy of Lebanon,' adds Hayate. 'There are more than just Palestinians who have been buried in the rubble of Beirut. Ninety per cent of the thousands dead in Lebanon are Lebanese civilians who didn't ask for war and had nothing to do with it.'

Ahlame comes into the kitchen with her friend/companion/ husband and a box of pastries, exclaiming:

'Sounds like a lot of discussion going on here! What have you made for us?'

Hayate, who is squeezing lemon for the hummus and baba-ghannouje, turns toward her. She is struck by Ahlame's beauty: she is suntanned and her hair and hazel eyes are more brilliant and larger than usual. Her mouth is bursting with sensuality. The details of her appearance reflect her taste in art nouveau – squared-off haircut and a dropped waist, off-the-shoulder dress, in a soft material printed with small flowers and golden leaves. And always the earrings, in the form of silver birds with their wings outspread, which clink with each movement of the head, with her smiles. Ahlame has such an expressive face and body! She does not appear conscious of her style, of the strength of her presence.

'You are so beautiful and full of life!' cries Hayate. 'One would never guess you had passed through the critical eye of the conference.'

'Oh! Me, I'm used to it now, but I was afraid for you. At one point, I wondered if you were going to be able to continue with all that criticism that had worn you down. You seemed so fragile.'

She puts her box on the table. Hadi pours a large glass of wine and wants to know who would like some. Hayate shows him the bottle she has brought: it's the whisky he likes – J&B – which in Beirut they have nicknamed Joumblatt-Berri.

'Are you drowning your sorrows in alcohol, Hadi?' Ahlame remarks. 'One would think I am the only one happy to be leaving. Ever since I reached my decision and the grant came through, I haven't been able to sit still. I am so anxious to breathe the air of freedom. Then I will be able to say what I think, get support for my ideas, and find people who understand me.'

Her lover, Tarek, watches her with a mixture of admiration, tenderness, resentment and fear. He looks overwhelmed. Hayate has learned that he will not be joining her in Paris. For several years, they have tried to have an open relationship, in which each partner agrees to a sexual freedom that they either admit to the other or hide from them. They have decided to accept it, even if it hurts them and makes them suffer. It does not appear to be working very well. It is an abstract utopia: to eliminate the spirit of possession and jealousy, to be free and accept the freedom of the other person to construct a relationship based on non-traditional values. In reality, tension in the relationship is accentuated. Power struggles appear and make the feelings of possession and jealousy come out, feelings which have not been eliminated, just the opposite! Instead of getting closer, they are separated by distrust and resentment. Instead of helping one another to develop their love harmoniously, deep trenches of misunderstanding are dug between the partners, who feel abandoned, replaced, belittled and undervalued.

Hayate has noticed that often it was the women who were more injured in the relationship, even when they had pushed for the experience. In general, men seemed to be able to live with this type of relationship more easily. Did they ask themselves fewer questions concerning the consequences of their actions, accept the present moment for what it is, without worrying about the other? Were they capable of a greater selfishness? Was it their education, social and family pressures, or the effect of culture and religion that authorised more freedom and less remorse with regard to the other's suffering? It seems as if they have always had the ability to compartmentalise their life and their partners, in a rational manner, with the appearance of not worrying about the emotional side, nor about wounds inflicted by actions and words. Did these differences between men and women have to do with the image, created by history, the culture, or with the gender – the physical, sexual differences? Nature? Or culture?

Hayate goes up to Ahlame and puts an arm around her shoulders.

'Yes, I am sad to leave. I have grown attached to this country and to dear friends like you. I know we'll see each other again, but when? What will happen to us in the meantime? How will we find each other? All of this distresses me. If I could tell myself that everything was going well for all of you, that you have found your path, that you are all happy, I would leave with a light heart.'

'We feel the same way about you,' Aïda interjects. 'If we were sure that you were leaving for a place, a job, a love that is right for you, that satisfies you, we wouldn't feel as worried as we do about your departure.'

Hadi has just put a tape into the player, a song by Marcel Khelifeh about Beirut: 'Baïroute, ya Baïroute'. The nostalgic accents of the melody, the tragic and poignant lyrics tell of the destruction of a city that is loved and tormented. All of the distress of the world seems to pour from the warm, profound and melancholy voice of Marcel Khelifeh; the *oude* gives it a grave rhythm which accentuates despair.

Hadi has finished preparing his dishes, he sits in a corner of the living room. Glass in hand, he broods over his sadness. Rima, who has just arrived with Tunisian pastries, looks at them all and shakes her head:

'It feels like a funeral here! I thought we were going to relax and have fun today, forget all our worries!'

She goes into the kitchen where Halima is still making her méchouïa. Hayate follows her, takes the box from her hands and arranges the cakes on a plate.

'That smells so good!' says Rima. 'I'm starving.'

'We were waiting for Sihame in order to start,' says Aïda. 'I'm happy to see you looking so well.'

'Sihame doesn't want us to wait for her. She'll be very late. She's finishing an article that she has to give in before coming.'

'Let's eat then!' suggests Aïda. 'Everyone is hungry.'

She gives out the plates and bread. They each serve themselves and go and sit in the living room. Hadi puts on another tape – a popular song by Faïrouze: 'Sa narji'ou yaoumane' – 'we will return one day'. The return of the Lebanese and the Palestinians. For the Palestinians, going back to a country from which they were taken; for the Lebanese, a return to a country destroyed, devastated and pillaged. The expressive, emotional voice of Faïrouze grows louder and overwhelms the living room with a call to love and reconciliation. Hayate has often wondered how a voice, a song, a melody and the beautiful, moving lyrics of Faïrouze have not yet succeeded in uniting the Arabs, in making them forget their quarrels and bitterness, in making them work for the betterment of their countries and the world. She is convinced that music has the extraordinary power to transform customs, values, current world institutions, if only one is ready to listen, ready to be changed! Unfortunately, political games and economic and financial mechanisms leave little room for music, art and culture.

Everyone here has understood the importance of music and art. Each one, in a personal way, has integrated it into their life. They – men and women – are all creators in their own way. Hadi paints pictures of destruction, violence, ruins and sorrow crossed by kites, rainbows, birds of peace and of return. Aïda, Halima and Ahlame express their suffering and joy through dance, song, writing. Their daughters are already following the example of their mothers; they are beginning to learn music and dance. Tarek produces films about the deprived, the dispossessed to whom he gives a voice, an expression of life and love. Rima and Sihame make journalism into an art through which they propose further dialogue, other images, other facts, another view of the current situation. Rania and Souheil have developed the art of living together, a rare and wonderful harmony.

The dishes are almost finished. There was not an abundance of food, but enough to make an occasion of it. Hayate clears the plates. Halima brings in the cakes. Aïda prepares her famous tea that she flavours with the leaf of a particular geranium from her garden. Hayate adores this tea which smells of honey, rose and violet. The children rush for the chocolate and cream pastries. There are also Tunisian cakes made of almond paste that Hayate loves.

Halima brings in her lute and announces a surprise. Everyone gathers around her, settling themselves on the rug, the cushions, on chairs.

'I have worked on a song for Hayate; I'd like us to sing it together. It's the song she brought us last year when she stopped in Tunis. It moved me, and I translated it into Arabic and adapted the music to the Arab lyrics.'

Hayate is touched by this gesture. She knew that several women in the group appreciated her music, but that one of them went to the trouble of putting a song into Arabic and on the *oude* fills her with happiness. Halima plucks the strings of the lute with one hand, and with the other, beats a rhythm. The quarter tones of the lute – the guitar only has half tones – subtly mark the music, making it more complex and melancholy in the minor tones. The syncopated rhythm breaks the monotony of the repetition. The soft, sensual voice of Halima rises. Her interpretation of a song about Lebanon, about the city, about unifying Beirut, about reconstructing it and bringing it back, about women standing up and liberating themselves; about people returning to hope, is admirable. Others take up the chorus, sing about the beloved city, the beloved woman, the beloved man, rebuilt on ruins, in streets finally cleared of cannons and militia. The children clap their hands, emphasising the joy of newfound peace.

Hayate is very touched, near to tears, by this gift made for her with so much grace and harmony. There are sometimes marvellous and intense moments where the friendship of those closest is almost physically perceptible. Hayate is experiencing one of those moments.

Then Ahlame suggests giving one of her performances. She stands in the middle of the group and pirouettes on her heels. Her dress whirls in great waves of silk. She traces, underlines and retraces the circles and the swirls of cloth carried along by her body, the image of what encircles her, holds her captive. She speaks of her childhood, her adolescence, her adult woman's life, her illusions and dreams, her sorrows and anguish. She expresses her experiences in large body gestures. She raises her arms to form other graceful and relaxed circles, tilts her head to one side and then the other; her body moves, walks, talks, vacillates, hesitates and begins its walk and speech again. Her red mouth forms a circle to declare:

> I have played heads and tails with my body
> Played hide and seek with the truth
> juggled the balls of despair
> Whirled until dizzy in the midst of both of you
> I have discovered the solitude of unequal sharing

174

the bitterness of tears no one cares about
the wounding of deceitful words
that one speaks as if a game
begun carefree
ended in the cruelty of emptiness
I who believed that it was true
hid my head in the hollow of your shoulder
out of fear that you might see my fear
my desperate jealousy
But you were no longer there to reassure me
Your hands on my hair caressed the head of the
    other
the one hitched to our limping carriage
from where will I draw the courage to stand up
and confront the fear of dizzying freedom
to raise my head and look straight at the sun as . . .
a mirror that passes?
I seek love, friendship
a loyal tenderness to give me strength
I see only a long black tunnel
without end, without exit
without reassuring light
without friends' hands to guide me
Where is the essential?
Where has the bird fallen, thrown from its cage?
What good is despair when one is always there?

In the picture Ahlame is painting, there is distress, anguish, a sadness that counters the happiness of departure she spoke of earlier. Through her art, she is able to say what she hides deep inside herself, even from close friends.

She is making an appeal and there is a detached look in her eye that focuses on her madness, her need for absolutes, her search for an ideal. She gives the impression of walking a tightrope on which she is losing her balance. Hayate senses uneasiness, an intense and inexplicable pain.

Happily, Aïda relaxes the atmosphere by dancing in the circle. Hadi has put the tape of a popular Tunisian song in the cassette player. Aïda has wrapped a long multi-coloured scarf round her hips. She gives herself over to the dance with all her being, as when she dives into a wave, or abandons herself to the hadra, or as she walks along a tree-lined street, or runs on fine sand, making one body with the Earth she loves and which takes her in. Within her there is so much imagination, sensuality, fantasy. She expresses freedom, an openness to the world and to others, the joy of being alive and knowing how to love. Her sense of rhythm is subtle, filled with poetry.

> She is beautiful
> a beauty which plunges its roots into the earth
> She is alive
> with a life that tells of the joy of loving
> She is sweet
> with a penetrating sweetness like the perfume of
> violets
> She is strong
> with a strength that affirms a space
> 'a room of her own'
> patiently constructed
> She is calm
> with a serenity that can no longer be taken away
> She is impassioned
> thirsty with the madness of creation

18

The following summer Hayate is in Paris. She receives a telephone call from Aïda in transit at Roissy Airport. She is en route for a conference on film in the United States. They will meet in Greece for a conference on women the following week. Their wish that they should see each other occasionally in different parts of the world is coming true.

Aïda's voice is charged with emotion and distress:

'I only have a few minutes before boarding. Listen, something awful has just happened. Ahlame is in the emergency ward of a hospital in Paris. Try to go and visit her and you can tell me how she is doing when we get to Greece.'

'An accident?'

'I really don't know. The people responsible for the boarding house where she was staying say that she jumped out of a window. Her family thinks she has fallen.'

Aïda's voice is racked with sobs.

'I have to hang up, the passengers are boarding already. Try to find out what has happened. If she leaves the hospital, she will need your help. Here is the address.'

She has just enough time to give Hayate the name of the hospital. A click; they've been cut off; and Hayate is left shattered. She thought Ahlame had already returned to Tunis. A year has passed since they left each other after the party at Aïda's place. Hayate had gone to teach in the U.S. and continued to correspond with Aïda. The letters they wrote to each other had helped them bear the separation. Aïda had told her that things were not going well for Ahlame. She had not found feminist groups or friends who truly understood her and encouraged her research, but she was studying theatre and cinema, two subjects she loved, and was looking forward to returning in order to write and work and put her ideas into action.

Hayate had written a letter to Ahlame, asking her for permission to use a part of her talk in an article. Ahlame's response, which was very moving, disenchanted, sad, should have warned her. She spoke of her loneliness, of disillusionment regarding France and French feminist movements, of racism she was encountering on a daily basis, of the great indifference of the West. She said that she felt she was sinking into anonymity which weighed upon her like a stone around her neck, and she was becoming depressed. Hayate's letter, which arrived just when she needed to hear the voice of a friend, had brought her out of her depression. She had also written a long paragraph about the identity of women – her own identity in particular. Hayate had not grasped the meaning of all of it: something about a history of naming, name of the father, husband, first name, pseudonym. Ahlame was researching her own name, her own identity. Her life in France must have disturbed her greatly for the detail of a name to take on such great proportions. The name is a symbol, the sign of what one is or would like to be, how one thinks one is perceived by others. It is the incarnation of the image reflected by the mirror, by others, by life. Hayate should have been more attentive to this allegory of the name expressed in the tormented lines of Ahlame. She is angry that she did not listen more fully to the distress of her friend. Maybe she could have helped her, stopped her from plunging into despair.

Hayate remembers her performances, and in particular the sketch she had interpreted at Aïda's house. What distress she was expressing even then! Hayate remembers the uneasiness, the fear, the vertigo which had gripped her upon seeing this tunnel of despair conveyed through Ahlame's art. Even so, Hayate had told herself that artistic expression would save her. Because she exorcised sorrow by personifying it, she would find the means to overcome it. She was wrong! Ahlame was much more fragile than she appeared. Her letter had ended: 'I feel bad. I'm afraid. There is no one here. Where are you?' Hayate feels guilty for not having responded to this call by offering more help.

Hayate calls the hospital and asks for the emergency ward. Where is Ahlame? Would she be able to talk to her? At the end of a few minutes which felt like hours, she gets hold of a nurse: Ahlame is in intensive care; they do not know if she will live. Could she have visitors? Not yet, not today. She must call again.

Hayate collapses as if she herself had fallen from the balcony. She trembles and dissolves into tears. She feels panic-stricken. What can she do? Who could she speak to? She picks up the phone and calls her close friend:

'Hello, what's going on? Your voice is shaky.'

In a few words, she sums up the situation.

'Calm down, *chérie*. There is nothing to do now but wait. You shouldn't be alone. Do you want to meet in a café to talk?'

They arrange a meeting. Paris, in this season, takes on a sensational beauty. The air is clear and fresh, the streets animated. The tranquil and majestic Seine offers its benches to lovers, to all those who seek a current of peaceful freedom. Hayate crosses a bridge which takes her to the Latin Quarter. She walks along quickly; she feels as if she's being watched. Usually she loves to look around her. There are so many fascinating things to observe in the streets of Paris – the way people dress, expressions, scenes, snatches of conversation, the lively atmosphere, the diversity of the people. But today she is preoccupied, troubled, turned inward.

She meets her friend in a small café. They cling to each other in silence. She loves this friend who understands her silence, and still finds the words for things both simple and complicated. They share work and have a common dream. They have similar imaginations and their questions come together, are linked in meaning. Today they do not speak. They hold hands, drink coffee, smoke a cigarette. Then they walk along the Seine under a sun which fades into the approaching night. Hayate shivers; she is troubled by the idea of being alone. In such moments, her solitude weighs her down like a yoke around her neck.

She calls the hospital every day. Two days later, they give her some hope. Ahlame will be able to leave. She is beginning to

179

respond to the treatment. Yes, she could have visitors. Hayate asks her friend Martine to accompany her. She does not have the courage to go alone. She buys a bouquet of flowers and meets Martine at the metro, near the hospital. It is a very warm day, already the beginning of summer.

They enter the emergency and intensive care units. The flowers, which are not allowed in this place where the sick are between life and death, are taken away. Hayate did not know this. This taking of the flowers makes her conscious of the serious nature of the illness. She squeezes Martine's hand to give herself courage. This section of the hospital is morbid. They let them enter the room.

Ahlame is on a bed in the middle of the room. Tubes penetrate several parts of her body. She is completely pale, almost blue, barely recognisable. Her eyes are closed. Doctors and nurses encircle the bed, controlling, calculating, measuring, observing the heart beats, the pulse, blood pressure, temperature, the smallest changes, the slightest variations. Tables and graphs surround the bed.

Hayate sees Martine's reaction to the scene: she can hardly bear the sight of it and the smell of medication. Hayate is seized with fright and takes a step back. But Ahlame's delicate face fascinates her, draws her forward again. She approaches her, with her white face on a white sheet, bruised body. She passes a hand over her eyes and kisses her gently on the forehead.

'Ahlame, it's me, Hayate!' she murmurs in her ear.

At the mention of these names, Ahlame quivers. She opens her eyes, eyes which turn in their deep sockets, ringed with shadows; her gaze comes from far off, a gaze which is already fading. Had she seen her? She winces a painful smile. Her mouth tries to form words. She murmurs sounds that are barely audible. Hayate tries to understand. She reads on her lips, listens, hears:

'The story of the mouse and the mountain, do you know it? The mountain was stronger than the mouse . . . I don't want to hurt my family . . . I don't want them to know . . . It's only you who can understand . . . the mouse . . . the mountain . . .'

180

Already, her eyes are closed against the pain. Hayate tries in vain to make Ahlame return to her, to hear her again, to reassure her that all of this is but a bad moment, a terrible dream, a nightmare that waking will deliver her from, that everything will be as before, that Ahlame will be full of life, love, will recite her poetry, perform her moving and expressive sketches again. Ahlame is still. The effort has exhausted her as if she had performed a hundred times. For the moment, she is resting. Will she ever have the strength to return? Hayate is not sure. She feels as if she has attended a final farewell, as if Ahlame was walking away on tip-toe, after having told her what she kept at the depths of her heart and did not dare reveal to anyone.

Hayate cries gently. She cannot tear herself away from this face of suffering, this martyred body, this bed – a symbol of the oppression and despair of women. A sensitive doctor watches her. He approaches, anxious and concerned:

'You shouldn't cry, she is doing much better. A few days ago, it was desperate. Now, she is practically out of danger. If she continues to make progress in this way, she'll be fine. Be happy! Those we see in such a frightful state rarely return to life. She must be very strong to resist death as she does.'

Hayate thanks him for his caring attention. She asks how long Ahlame will be in this room, and in the hospital. If she continues to improve at the same rate, she should be out of intensive care at the end of the week, four or five days maximum. As for the hospital stay, it is uncertain. Everything depends on her – three, six months, a year possibly! Ahlame has a paralysed back, with no reaction in her legs. Her spinal column was injured and it's serious. But there is no cause for panic. This afternoon, he noticed a small movement in one of her feet. That is a good sign.

Hayate thanks him. She looks at Ahlame once more. Ever since she has spoken, she has not moved. A nurse comes up and thanks her for having said a few words to Ahlame. It is excellent that she was able to communicate. That is a good development; it proves the importance of her being there, Ahlame's need to see her. Since her arrival in the hospital, she had not spoken. The nurse asks

181

Hayate if she will be back. Hayate responds that unfortunately she is leaving for Greece the next day. As soon as she is back in Paris, she will return for a visit.

She leaves the room, very affected by the visit. Fortunately, Martine has accompanied her. They support each other, talk together, discuss other moments in their lives, moments of struggle against despair and the desire for suicide. At that time, they were both in the United States. Hayate had just fled from the ancestral customs of her country, a society which did not permit women to take a new, creative path, arranged marriages, a family which stifled her as much by their attention as by their rules, and a church which valued rites more than faith, rules above grace.

Martine had also fled her country, France, and laws which, at the time, punished abortion; she fled also from a strict mother who did not allow her freedom. At eighteen, she married a soldier who promised her a life in America, a dream of many young people of her age. She found herself, not in the land of Hollywood or Disneyland, but in a godforsaken place in the midwest, in the midst of cornfields. Her husband was no longer the handsome soldier who had seduced her with his uniform and accent; he was a worker at a General Motors factory. Alone and a foreigner in a small, isolated town in Indiana, she was the 'Frenchy' that everyone stared at, wide-eyed, the 'Froggy' on whom everyone projected their fantasies of loose living. She did not dare leave the house for fear of being watched or followed. Shut up in her square soulless, house, she had tried several times to open her veins. It was then that she met Hayate.

It was a day in autumn. She had been invited to speak to a French class in the college of a small town, the college where Hayate both studied and taught French. That day Hayate had felt the same surprise as when she met Aïda and Ahlame for the first time. That magical instant of unusual encounters when you know that a great friendship is starting to form. She remembers still: Martine was wearing a black leather suit, her black hair fell straight down on her shoulders, eye-liner accentuated her black eyes. For Hayate, she personified existentialism, which fascinated and attracted her, which symbolised freedom – France, Paris – a country, a city she did not know, of which she used to dream. Martine had seen in her the Mediterranean, the beaches, the waves, the sea that symbolises flight. Ever since their first meeting, they would call each other for hours on end and they would meet during weekends to talk. They always had a thousand things to say to each other. Their friendship saved them from loneliness and despair. They had the impression they had always known each other. They found in one another the call of adventure, the call of the unknown, the call to transcend the self, the call of dreams and the ideal.

Why is death so attractive when one is young? What could have been so intolerable and insurmountable for Ahlame that she took this step towards it? What did the mountain she talked of represent? Was she comparing herself to the mouse? Was she speaking of lost illusions? Was she making an allusion to France, to racism, to Tunisia, to women's movements, to the cruelty of the world in general? Was she saying how impossible it is for some weak people even though they are overflowing with imagination, to overcome trials, to rise above despair in order to attain knowledge and wisdom? Was it for this that she had tried to throw herself into final oblivion?

One does not measure death when one is young, any more than one measures life. Governments take advantage of this to enrol young people in armies, to send them to their death. They throw themselves into the adventure without thinking. Would they jump into this murderous insanity if they knew what was waiting for them? Would one refuse birth with a knowledge of life? When one is young and full of dreams, one does not weigh things up. Passion, enthusiasm, the desire to know and discover give rise to dazzling actions, but the despair is just as searing. One must keep the momentum of creative madness without giving in to the dizziness of death. In her diary, Hayate draws the waves and the sea of Tunisia with a great red sun, a tree and the village train. She knows she will find them again one day.

183